ECONOMIC ISSUES, PROBL

SERVICE ENTITIES IN OPEN-CLOSED INNOVATION

ECONOMIC ISSUES, PROBLEMS AND PERSPECTIVES

Additional books in this series can be found on Nova's website under the Series tab.

ECONOMIC ISSUES, PROBLEMS AND PERSPECTIVES

SERVICE ENTITIES IN OPEN-CLOSED INNOVATION

YUMIKO KINOSHITA

Nova Science Publishers, Inc.
New York

For permission to use material from this book please contact us:
Telephone 631-231-7269; Fax 631-231-8175
Web Site: http://www.novapublishers.com

NOTICE TO THE READER

The Publisher has taken reasonable care in the preparation of this book, but makes no expressed or implied warranty of any kind and assumes no responsibility for any errors or omissions. No liability is assumed for incidental or consequential damages in connection with or arising out of information contained in this book. The Publisher shall not be liable for any special, consequential, or exemplary damages resulting, in whole or in part, from the readers' use of, or reliance upon, this material. Any parts of this book based on government reports are so indicated and copyright is claimed for those parts to the extent applicable to compilations of such works.

Independent verification should be sought for any data, advice or recommendations contained in this book. In addition, no responsibility is assumed by the publisher for any injury and/or damage to persons or property arising from any methods, products, instructions, ideas or otherwise contained in this publication.

This publication is designed to provide accurate and authoritative information with regard to the subject matter covered herein. It is sold with the clear understanding that the Publisher is not engaged in rendering legal or any other professional services. If legal or any other expert assistance is required, the services of a competent person should be sought. FROM A DECLARATION OF PARTICIPANTS JOINTLY ADOPTED BY A COMMITTEE OF THE AMERICAN BAR ASSOCIATION AND A COMMITTEE OF PUBLISHERS.

Additional color graphics may be available in the e-book version of this book.

LIBRARY OF CONGRESS CATALOGING-IN-PUBLICATION DATA

Kinoshita, Yumiko.
  Service entities in open-closed innovation / Yumiko Kinoshita.
      p. cm. -- (Economic issues, problems and perspectives)
  Includes index.
  ISBN 978-1-61209-312-3 (softcover)
  1. Service industries--Technological innovations. 2. Service industries--Information technology. I. Title.
  HD9980.5.K564 2011
  338'.064--dc22
                          2011003570

Published by Nova Science Publishers, Inc. † New York

CONTENTS

PREFACE

The service sector amounts to 70-75% of the global economy in advanced countries. However, there is far less empirical and statistical studies performed with regard to the service sector than manufacturing sector. The productivity of the service sector has not been identified clearly in relation to the sectoral growth because the productivity of service sectors has not been improved for decades in major OECD countries. The growth of service sectors are important particularly from the viewpoint of small to medium-sized enterprises (SMEs), which consist a large part of the service sector even more than that of manufacturing sector. From major statistics and previous literatures, this chapter addresses the role of SMEs in the development of today's economy, leading to structural changes in the service sector. To achieve economic development, it is important to consider the introduction of Information Technology (IT) and the development of expertise knowledge, by either internally, externally, or with public support, that aim to improve productivity. In this regard, Knowledge-intensive services (KIS) have a special role to play for facilitating productivity in the service economy. The impact of service research and development (R&D) is also focused in recent researches. In line with these trends, this chapter aims at arguing economic growth models for SMEs, in which R&D activities promote and transform innovation in the service sector with the appropriate use of KIS and IT services. By incorporating business size dimension, the firm-level panel data analysis successfully reveals that a balanced combination of IT investment and KIS inputs achieve steady turnover growth for service sectors from both micro and macro perspectives. In addition, service intermediate inputs play a moderator role against fluctuations in the entire economy. Service R&D gives a certain impact on revenue trends although firm age, business size, and sectoral aspects in addition to the balance of tangible and intangible assets are related to the effectiveness of R&D activities. In conclusion, it is critically important for future economic directions and policies to remember that the balanced investment into IT and KIS will promote the growth of the entire economy through the development of SMEs by means of structural changes and innovations associated with the service-oriented economy.

Chapter 1

INTRODUCTION

SERVICE ECONOMY AND THE ROLE OF INNOVATION IN SERVICES[1]

Service is a primary growth driver for the present world market as the tertiary sector of the economy. The term, *service*, has a variety of associations and annotations as we aim to analyze its meaning, role, impact, and functionality in the contexts of the present and future economy. Economic trends surrounding service consider the question from the point of view of scientific knowledge and its creation. Albert Einstein once says, "*it might appear that there are no essential methodological differences between astronomy and economics…but in reality such methodological differences do exist. The discovery of general laws in the field of economics is made difficult by the circumstance that observed economic phenomena are often affected by many factors, which are very hard to evaluate separately. In addition, the experience which has accumulated since the beginning of the so-called civilized period of human history has…been largely influenced and limited by causes which are by no means exclusively economic in nature*" (1949).

The importance of service has been recognized in a number of statistical sources, which clearly show the degree of its contribution to the growth of the global economy as well as fluctuations in the current market. According to the World Bank, most of the job losses were seen in the manufacturing sector in

---

[1] In this chapter, 'the service sector' refers to the collection of non-manufacturing sectors as a whole in contrast to 'the manufacturing sector.' Each sector in the service sector is mentioned as 'service sector(s).' Each service-related activity or service as a product is expressed as 'service(s).'

previous financial crises, but employment increased in services on average (2008, 2009). During this crisis of 2009, however, there have been substantial employment losses in service sectors primarily due to the serious impact on the trends of financial sector services, real estate and construction. Poverty is also expected to expand, or take a slower exit in a number of developing countries (World Bank, 2008, 2009). Sophisticated algorithms for designing financial products and distributing risks in a combination of them are one of the derivatives of accumulated technical and expertise knowledge in the said area (International Monetary Fund, 2009a, 2009b; Dekle, Eaton, & Kortum, 2008), having the impact of supportive technologies on the delivered services remain to be clarified.

Einstein also mentions that *memory, the capacity to make new combinations, and the gift of oral communication have made possible development...(which) manifest themselves in...scientific and engineering accomplishments (and the like)...It is easy to raise (abovementioned) questions, but difficult to answer them with any degree of assurance* (1949). A part of our scientific and engineering knowledge is, as he refers to, structure of information and means of communication. Researchers attend to a variety of issues including the relationship of service and the economy, with some degrees of uncertainties, in complicated structural attributes that are both economic and non-economic as articulated by Aoki (2001) and Sudoh (2005).

The issue with regard to service has been articulated in many scientific fields in the past. Reviews on the service sector date back to the 1960s (Fuchs, 1965), being investigated thoroughly from the viewpoint of economic structural analysis. The service sector has also been analyzed in parallel with manufacturing in terms of measuring the degree of innovation, being referred to as 'service innovation' (Barras, 1986; Eurostat, 1992-2009; Finnish Funding Agency for Technology and Innovation (TeKes), 2006; Miles, 2006; NESTA Policy and Research Unit, 2008; OECD, 1996) in more recent years. Different perspectives have been offered from the fields of Information Technology (IT), engineering, business management, and sociology with the efforts of establishing an interdisciplinary field called 'service science' (Hidaka, 2006; IBM). In these efforts, the structures of information pertaining to service have presented multi-layered perspectives (Kinoshita & Sudoh, 2008) to those who would like to take a deeper look at the nature of service. Furthermore, the understanding of these concepts will help to have an overview of the future development of the service sector, leading us to the management of innovation and values generated in the service sector in a flexible, dynamic, and effective manner.

Starting from the structural analysis on the service sector to find an answer for a number of economic questions, which have already been presented years ago, such as elasticity of substitution, factor prices, intermediaries used in service, and idiosyncratic parameters of consumers (Fuchs, 1965), the ones addressed in recent years are the role of supporting technologies and its relation to expertise knowledge used to deliver diversified services (Finnish Funding Agency for Technology and Innovation (TeKes), 2007a; Miles, 2005; 2008). According to Eurostat, for instance, 43% of Science and Technology jobs in EU 27 countries are in the service sector (Eurostat, 2007). Not only global services but also locally traded services will be subject to systemic research and development (R&D) activities more than before (European Commission, 2008; Wolfl, 2005). The clarification of geographical locality, substitution of products, and heterogeneity of knowledge in the service sector are historical but ongoing problems for economists, out of which the degree of technology and knowledge intensiveness in services and the effective utilization of IT (Finnish Funding Agency for Technology and Innovation (TeKes), 2007b) are the front end of the spectrum.

The investment into 'knowledge' in general refers to the amount of input into R&D, education, and software besides the investment into capital including tangibles and intangibles (OECD, 2008b). These investments by themselves are a part of service activities. The issue of R&D in the service sector has been brought up to the table for discussion to find appropriate deflators for measuring the impact of service R&D accurately, and to discover the mechanism of sectoral and productivity growth (Djellal, Francoz, Gallouj, Gallouj, & Jacquin, 2003; Freeman & Soete, 2007; Fukao, 2007; Hall, 2007; National Science Foundation and National Institute of Standards and Technology, 2005; Nomura, 2004; OECD, 1980, 1996, 2005b; Timmer, O'Mahony, & Ark, 2007; Young, 1996). To transform the service sector based on potential innovativeness of knowledge generated through service, it is suggested furthermore that increasing connection and adoption of service-related technologies in other research fields, such as IT, genomics, and neurosciences, should be pursued (Atkinson & Castro, 2008; Atkinson & Wial, 2008; Council on Competitiveness, 2004; European Commission, 2008; NESTA Policy and Research Unit, 2008; PREST, TNO, ARCS, and SERVILAB, 2006). To respond to these challenges, a critical issue is how we deal scientifically with the creation of knowledge, its process to evolve into the innovation in service, and the contribution to the growth of productivity and total output in the service sector.

These issues stand at the crossroads of economics and informatics as it aims to consider the interpretation of economic entities and the creation of structured information in relation to the heterogeneity of technologies, namely IT, from the viewpoint of innovation in service (Atkinson & Wial, 2008; Forge, Blackman, Bohlin, & Cave, 2009; OECD, 2008c; Scott, 1999). In other words, this is a question regarding the state space for the creation of knowledge and its impact on total output. Simply enough, the reason why the growth of productivity leads to the increase of output has not been proved yet, which this research will be concerned with by articulating the nature of information and networks (Sudoh, 2005) as vital components for the analysis of innovation in service from the perspectives of knowledge, followed by empirical and qualitative studies. Furthermore, as we have witnessed in the financial crisis from 2009, the direction of future IT services and networking technologies, currently serving as a part of utilities for our daily lives (Buyya, Yeo, & Venugopal, 2008; Rimal, Eunmi, & Lumb, 2009), has a huge impact on the course of the entire service sector to take for years ahead.

In addition, the number of smaller firms is increasing in the service economy. It is suggestive that the study on the development of the service sector is useful and effective as well as necessary for the issue of economic development for developing countries (Kinoshita, 2009a). The discussion on the size of firms is important in terms of finding the optimal scale of investment into IT system, and how we can design innovation system and policies for which a certain sector of the economy and a part of the population are allocated. According to statistics in U.S., U.K. and Japan where service sectors have been relatively developed well, it is clarified that the Pareto distribution is shifted in service sectors compared to manufacturing in terms of business size. OECD (2008a, 2008d) also mentions that small to medium-sized enterprises (SMEs) are facing a structural change in the global economy, and that the role of SMEs is becoming important in the service economy, which we must perform detailed analysis.

To return to a sustainable growth from the financial turmoil (Dekle, Eaton, & Kortum, 2008; World Bank, 2008), being as a short-term objective of economic activities, it is suggested from a longer perspective that the model for promoting the expansion of service sector should be studied further as we acknowledge the impact of information structure, being expressed in knowledge, inter alia, the effects of key technologies to play to that end, first and foremost, IT and other emerging and critical technological fields, such as biotechnology (Second OECD Ad Hoc Meeting on Biotechnology Statistics, 2001), and the diffusion of potential impacts of the expanding service sector into the variations of productivity growth and earnings structure among firms (Cainelli, Evangelista, & Savona, 2006; Griffith, Harrison, & Van Reenen, 2006; Koellinger, 2008). It is assumed that the factor for the growth of service sector is the existence of multiple technological fields, which allows for endogenous development of knowledge, achieving a shift in productivity distributions among firms.

Innovation can be examined according to technological development phases. One way to describe economic phases is the life cycle of a technology system. It takes the following six steps: (1) the laboratory-invention phase with early applications in small scale, (2) the demonstration of technical and commercial feasibility with wide potential applications, (3) growth phase with structural, political and regulatory changes, (4) high growth with a wide acceptance of technology in leading economies, (5) profitability decline with challenges of new technologies, and (6) maturity stage with the possibility of co-existence with new technologies or slow disappearance (Freeman & Louca, 2001; Freeman & Soete, 1997).

Trends of current business in IT sector, the optimal scale of investment into IT by businesses, and the evolution of IT services are standard points to be investigated, which can be associated with the foregoing points of discussion in terms of the behavior of service sector. As for the innovation in service, in particular, there are several models presented which explain the development phases of service in terms of quality, availability, and the like (Lages & Fernandes, 2005; Service Innovation Research Initiative, 2009; Zeithaml, Parasuraman, & Berry, 1990). A major example is Community Innovation Survey in European Union (Eurostat, 1992-2009). In such an existing framework of analysis, the issue of innovation is addressed typically as an environmental and complex structural attributes associated with diverse innovation systems. Freeman and Soete (2007) state that we should reconstruct our understanding on major economic indexes including Gross Domestic Product (GDP) due to the rise of the service economy.

From the perspectives of business sizes, geographical elements, having been addressed by Krugman, Fujita and many others (Asheim & Gertler, 2005; Audretsch & Feldman, 1996; Coe, Helpman, and Hoffmaister, 2009; Fujita, Krugman, and Venables, 2001; Jonathan & Samuel, 2002; Kranich, 2009; Krugman, 1997), must be considered in terms of productivity and opportunities for creating new services (Miozzo & Soete, 2001) through the activities of SMEs. The geospatial elements achieve two goals: to increase return on investment per area and to gain competitiveness in a global market by overcoming locality. To support these objectives, IT is used to create access to local entities as well as actors in the global market for improving productivity (Basu & Fernald, 2006; Bresnahan, Brynjolfsson, & Hitt, 2002; Jorgenson, Ho, & Stiroh, 2003; Scott, 1999; Shapiro, Varian, & Farrel, 2004; Stiroh, 2002). From micro-level perspective firms are required to enhance the degree of expertise in the production and delivery of knowledge more to compete in the global market due to the increasing introduction and diffusion of IT (Dikaiakos, Katsaros, Mehra, Pallis, & Vakali, 2009; Yu, Li, Li, & Hong, 2004). This aspect is also applied to the activities performed by smaller firms (OECD, 2005a, 2008a). In recent years, in particular, the systemic R&D efforts in the field of service are increasing, and firms are exposed more to the competition intensified to generate new knowledge pertaining to service, making them more knowledge and technology intensive (European Commission, 2008; Miles, 2005; OECD, 2006).

In addition, as Coase (1937) mentioned, the existence of costs for information has been a reason for the establishment of firms and organizations. Due to the deepening integration of information technologies in economy and society, the costs for obtaining, managing, and utilizing information have been reduced, which allow for a new type of open organizational schemes to emerge. In such a situation, people are required to have knowledge and skills, in particular, to connect and negotiate with external organizations (Goldsmith & Eggers, 2004). Public administrative agencies have established more cooperative relationships with non-profit organizations (NPOs) and private firms so that the government ministries and agencies shall be capable of developing comprehensive services by organizing multi-level (national and local) consolidated services (Sudoh, 2005, 2006, 2008).

A large part of the transaction costs have been eliminated by automated technologies, leading to a decrease in the costs of partnership (Goldsmith & Eggers, 2004). According to Coase (1937), if partnership is more effective cost-wise than operating business on our own, more partnership, cooperation and outsourcing will be sought for. This propensity is also related to the trends of firm size and its turnover. Goldsmith et al. (2004) says that a system to deliver a service is properly designed and networked, in which it has a potential to create opportunities for different kinds of innovation. In line with this perspective, the innovation in service is going to be reviewed in a way that shows the diversification of profit structure at sectoral levels.

With these observations, this chapter deals with innovation specifically in service by articulating the needs for designing an analytical framework for service innovation to measure the impact on economic growth focusing on business sizes, and by referencing panel data models with some modifications to reflect the role of knowledge in the service economy more precisely. Focal points of analysis in this chapter are as follows. The first point of analysis is the impact on productivity among firms in the service sectors. Based on preliminary observation on data, it is clarified that the distribution of turnover and firm size is distinctive in the service sector from that of manufacturing sector, thus leading to different structures for sectoral growth and productivity improvement by firm size.

The second point is the role of investment into R&D in services in accordance with the roles of knowledge-intensive services (KIS) to play on productivity trends in relation to those of IT services. It aims to discuss the measurement methodology of investment into knowledge as the coordination of IT services and KIS to articulate its impact on elasticity of substitution of knowledge. For the entire discussion, IT is considered to be the foundation, or at least a major contributor, for creating new markets, improving productivity, and delivering services. In this chapter, the role of IT services and KIS are taken into account as two pillars to promote R&D in services and to achieve the innovation in service.

Firstly, the recent trends of the service sector in the world is overviewed so that the scope of analysis in later sections is narrowed down and articulated clearly. This step is taken to identify growing service sectors, and find what factors are related with the growth of service sectors. For these purposes, data on international economy are reviewed from structural perspectives. The relationship of macro economy and service sectors suggests that tertiary attainment and Information and Communication Technology (ICT) capital formation are correlated with the growth of service sectors while multi-factor productivity (MFP) and investment into knowledge are not related.

The empirical analyses refer to the models presented by Eaton, Helpman, and Kramarz (2009), Besanko and Doraszelski (2004), Pagano and Schivardi (2003), Acs and Audretsch (1988), Shefer and Frenkel (2005), Cohen and Klepper (1996), Koeller (2005), and Veugelers and Cassiman (2005). The firm size variations on output are examined, incorporating the effect of R&D in services (Duchêne, Lykogianni, & Verbeek, 2009; Jankowski, 2001; Young, 1996), by using Japanese firm-level financial data. The hypothesis to be analyzed is the shift of Pareto distribution among service sectors in that it is represented by the variations of profit structures by firm size. A thorough analysis on the relationship between firm size and turnover in the service sector has rarely been seen in previous literatures in economics. In particular, this analysis encompasses the impact of R&D in services, which is, by itself, a new topic for empirical analyses for the area of services.

Dynamic panel data models are used as a large amount of cross-section data are available while time-series data are short, in which lagged dependent variables appear in correlation with error term. Arellano et al. (1989; 2001), Hahn, Hausman, and Kuersteinerm (2002), Pakes and Ericson (1998), Pakes (2003), Ackerberg, Benkard, Berry, and Pakes (2007) and many others have approached to these issues using instrument variables (IV). This chapter focuses on structural parameters and imperfect instrument variables (IIV) based on Olley and Pakes (1996) and Ackerberg et al. (2007) incorporating the findings of Levinsohn and Petrin (2003), Bajari, Benkard, and Levin (2007), Andrews and Stock (2007), and Nevo and Rosen (2008). Details on methodology can be referred also to Kinoshita (2009a, 2009b). In this analysis, the relationship of knowledge spillover (Jaffe, Trajtenberg, & Fogarty, 2000), KIS, and the use of IT are focused. This analysis is conducted to find the impact of knowledge on the performance of firms by size variations so that the relationship of information and networks are clarified from the viewpoint of the innovation in service. In summary, this chapter deals with existing hypotheses on the relationship between firm size, its growth, and innovation by presenting a different scenario for the service sector than manufacturing by incorporating the role of service R&D into analysis in relation to the impact of IT and KIS.

Chapter 2

THE WORLD ECONOMY AND THE GROWTH IN SERVICE SECTORS

The following sections are concerned with, first of all, how the innovation of service has been generated and developed in the world economy, and which factors are important for the future economy to continue to promote the innovation in service. In particular, the role of R&D in services is focused, which has increased swiftly in recent years following the review on the role of IT and KIS in this process. The question of innovation is analyzed to clarify how the trends of the service sector have caused the variation of profit structures at a sectoral level in business size dimension.

1.1. GLOBAL TRENDS BY SECTOR

This section gives an overview of the service sector around the world to narrow down the scope of analysis to be described further in later sections. In the International Standard Industrial Classification (ISIC) Revision 2, services are defined as all activities in: 'Wholesale and retail trade and restaurants and hotels,' 'Transport, storage and communication,' 'Financial, insurance, real estate and business services,' and 'Community, social and personal services' (OECD, 2008b; United Nations Statistics Division). In ISIC Revision 3, services are defined more loosely including the following: 'Wholesale and retail trade; repair of motor vehicles, motorcycles and personal and household goods,' 'Hotels and restaurants,' 'Transport, storage and communications,' 'Financial intermediation,' 'Real estate, renting and business activities,'

'Public administration and defense; compulsory social security,' 'Education,' 'Health and social work,' 'Other community, social and personal service activities,' 'Private households with employed persons,' and 'Extra-territorial organizations and bodies.' In ISIC Revision 4, certain categories, such as 'Information and Communication' and 'Professional, scientific and technical activities,' become more distinctive (US Economic Classification Policy Committee, Statistics Canada, Mexico's Instituto Nacional de Estadistica, & Geografia e Informatica)[1].

Based on the sectoral classification above, the trend of service sectors with high growth rates, moderate growth rates, and lower growth rates are shown in Figure 1, Figure 2, and Figure 3 respectively. The aggregate of banks, insurance, real estate and other business services has been showing a steady growth over the last decade while the total of government, health, education and other personal services has exhibited a moderate or leveled growth. The aggregate of transport, trade, hotels and restaurantshas shown slower or negative growth rates. These growth trends seem fairly consistent across these major countries in the figures.

To see the relationships of the service sector with macro economy in further detail from structural aspects, historical data are examined starting from 1970 to the latest years available[2]. The relationships of the service sector with the macro indicators below are investigated in terms of gross national income per capita, exports of services, imports of services, shares of information and communication technologies (ICT)[3], investment in non-

---

[1] For details on industry classification, please also refer to North American Industry Classification System (NAICS) at http://www.census.gov/eos/www/naics/, UK Standard Industrial Classification of Economic Activities 2007 at http://www.statistics. gov.uk/statbase/Product.asp?vlnk=14012, and Statistics Bureau, Ministry of Internal Affairs and Communication of Japan at http://www.stat.go.jp/english/ data/service/2004/bunrui.htm. For further information on pricing of services, please refer to International Labor Organization (ILO) at http://www.imf.org/external/np/ sta/tegppi/index.htm, and transfer pricing for services at Japan's National Tax Agency. See http://www.nta. go.jp/foreign_language/08.pdf.

2 See Kinoshita (2009a) for collected figures.

3 The OECD definition of the ICT sector is found at http://www.oecd.org/ dataoecd/ 34/37/2771153.pdf. It includes the following 4-digit classes: Insulated wire cable (3130); Instruments and appliances for measuring, checking, testing, navigating and other purposes except industrial process equipment (3312); Industrial process equipment (3313); Wholesale of machinery, equipment and supplies (part only, where possible) (5150); Telecommunications (6420); Renting of office machinery and equipment (7123) as well as the following 2-digit industries: Office, accounting and computing machinery (30); Manufacture of radio, television and communication equipment and apparatus (32); and Computer and related activities (72).

residential gross fixed capital formation, Multi-factor productivity (MFP), investment in knowledge, tertiary attainment for age group 25-64, and participation of micro, small, and medium-sized enterprises (MSMEs)[4] in the economy as a number of companies.

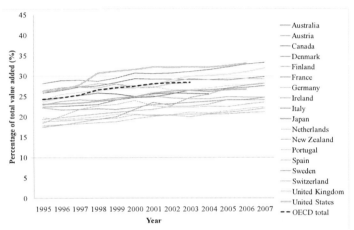

Note: 1) Data period: 1995-latest year available. 2) Industry classification: International Standard Industrial Classification of All Economic Activities Rev.3.1 (ISIC Rev.3.1). Financial intermediation (J) includes 65-Financial intermediation, except insurance and pension funding, 66-Insurance and pension funding, except compulsory social security, and 67-Activities auxiliary to financial intermediation. Real estate, renting and business activities (K) corresponds to 70-Real estate activities, 71-Renting of machinery and equipment without operator and of personal and household goods, 72-Computer and related activities, 73-Research and development, and 74-Other business activities. 3) Unit: Percentage of total value added.

Source: Created by author based on OECD Factbook -Economic, Environmental and Social Statistics (2009b).

Figure 1. Macroeconomic trends of services: value-added in banks, insurance, real estate and other business services[2] (%).

---

[4] Small and medium-sized enterprises (SMEs) are firms which employ fewer than a given number of employees. This number varies across countries, in which the most frequent upper limit is 250 employees, such as in the European Union. Some countries set the limit to 200 employees, while the United States considers SMEs to include firms with fewer than 500 employees. Small firms are generally those with fewer than 50 employees, while micro-enterprises have at most 10, or in some cases 5, workers. Financial assets are also used to define SMEs although in this chapter, these size classes are aligned with National Size Class (NSC 1-5), which corresponds to 1-9 (NSC1), 10-19 (NSC2), 20-99 (NSC3), 100-499 (NSC4), and 500+(NSC5) (OECD, 2002, 2005c, 2008b).

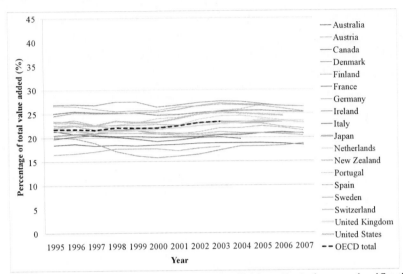

Note: 1) Data period: 1995-latest year available. 2) Industry classification: International Standard Industrial Classification of All Economic Activities Rev.3.1 (ISIC Rev.3.1). Public administration and defense; compulsory social security (L), Education (M), Health and social work (N), and Other community, social and personal service activities (O) are included. 3) Unit: Percentage of total value added.

Source: Created by author based on OECD Factbook -Economic, Environmental and Social Statistics (2009b).

Figure 2. Macroeconomic trends of services: value added in government, health, education and other personal services (%).

The growth of banks, insurance, real estate and other business services is positively related to all the indicators above except for MFP. With investment in knowledge, it is weakly related in a positive direction. The growth of government, health, education and other personal services is also related positively with the macro indicators in a similar way with the previous category of services. It is suggested that the degree of correlation is weaker than the previous category. In addition, the correlation with MFP is not observed. Please note that the relatively stronger correlations with investment into knowledge and tertiary attainment are caused due to the output of education included in this category.

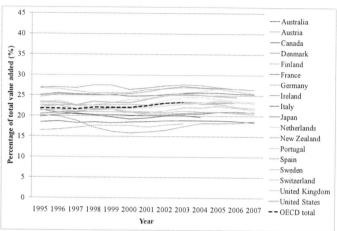

Note: 1) Data period: 1995-latest year available. 2) Industry classification: International Standard Industrial Classification of All Economic Activities Rev.3.1 (ISIC Rev.3.1). Wholesale and retail trade; repair of motor vehicles, motorcycles and personal and household goods (G), Hotels and restaurants (H), and Transport, storage and communications (I) are included. 3) Unit: Percentage of total value added.

Source: Created by author based on OECD Factbook -Economic, Environmental and Social Statistics (2009b).

Figure 3. Macroeconomic trends of services: value added in transport, trade, hotels and restaurants (%).

The macroeconomic indicators such as output quantity, price deflator, productivity, and capital accumulation must exhibit significant variations across sectors (OECD, 1996). As previously mentioned, input deflators and the unit of measurement for service output are still not defined in a consistent manner (Bosworth & Triplett, 2007; Corrado, Hulten, & Sichel, 2009; Triplett & Bosworth, 2004). However, common and persistent trends in the service sector of the three economies are: (i) The share of ICT-related services and financial services compose a large share of the service sector. (ii) The fastest growing sector, however, is business-related services, which are primarily known as knowledge-intensive services (KIS). (iii) Healthcare, education, and public sectors (including defense) show heterogeneous trends in terms of factors for growth. The following section deals with another common and persistent trend in the service sector across major OECD countries, which is the relationship between firm size and the turnover of service sectors.

There are several important points that are clarified in these data. Firstly, a part of service sectors contributes to the growth of output as well as the volume of trade both in export and import. Trade volume is growing particularly in European countries (especially within Europe) and Asian & Pacific countries (World Trade Organization, 2009). Secondly, the investment into ICT and educational level seem to be correlated to the growth rate of the service sector. The positive correlations of service sectors with total output and trade in addition to the investment into ICT and educational attainment seem consistent for the entire service sector.

In contrast, MFP does not correlate with any of these three service categories. Data do not show the correlation between the service sector and MFP even at a country level. It is suggestive that the issue of MFP may be investigated with care for each service sector potentially as an issue with input deflators and statistical methodologies (Amiti & Wei, 2005; Atkinson, 2009; Diewert, Greenlees, & Hulten, 2009; Dunham, 2003; Jensen, Kletzer, Bernstein, & Feenstra, 2005; Triplett & Bosworth, 2004). The other important point is the participation of SMEs in the service sector. It is clear that the existence of SMEs is correlated with the trend of service sector well. Data on SMEs at a country level show that the growth of service sector is positively related with the number of SMEs in the economy in all seventeen countries in analysis except for Japan.

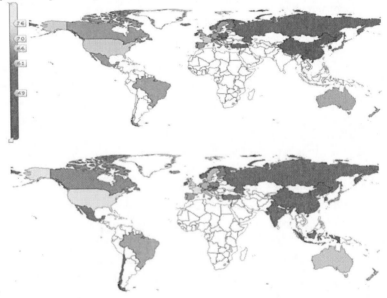

Note: Scale as a percentile of total value added.
Source: Figures are directly obtained from OECD (2009c) .

Figure 4. Real value-added in services in 1995 (top), 2000 (middle), and 2005 (bottom).

1.2. THE RELATIONSHIP OF FIRM SIZE AND PRODUCTIVITY

Partly as the previous observation has shown, the participation of SMEs in the service sector increases as the service sector grows in the economy. The growth rates of real value-added in services have been growing both in developed and developing countries. Meanwhile, how can we explain the stagnation of multi-factor productivity (MFP) growth that is commonly seen throughout the service sector in advanced countries? Is it possible to assume that the growth of the service sector can be achieved without a strong growth of productivity, meaning that primary growth factors are the input into capital and labor? This section is going to review this point by using data on the U.S., U.K., and Japan regarding turnover by sector and size of firm. It is also going to argue about the contradictory trend that is seen in the Japanese economy only, which is the negative correlation between the participation of SMEs and the growth of the service sector.

The relationship of firm size and productivity has been a proved concept in a number of empirical studies in the past, such as Besanko and Doraszelski (2004), Pagano and Schivardi (2003), Shefer and Frenkel (2005), and Veugelers and Cassiman (2005). Most recently, Eaton, Kortum, and Kramarz (2009) have proved that the number of firms and the profit of an industry do correlate, showing a Pareto distribution. These findings are based on the hypothesis that the firm size variation can be used as a proxy for the productivity distribution. This distribution is normally described as in Figure

5. These previous researches have been proved, with an occasional counterfactual finding, for example, Career and Thurik (1998, 2000), by using data in manufacturing sectors.

Krugman (1989), Melitz (2003), Ottaviano and Melitz (2008), and Chaney (2008) discussed the issue of elasticity of substitution in terms of trade margin. Krugman (1989) argued that when the elasticity is high, the margin of export becomes high. On the other hand, Chaney (2008) discusses that a decreasing cost will increase the impact on trade flow when the elasticity of substitution is *low* and firms are heterogeneous, that scarcely substitutable products will be replaced less in the market, and that productive firms will become more sensitive to a change in fixed cost when market is open. These theoretical and empirical findings are important in that the relationship between the elasticity of substitution and firm's market share is expressed.

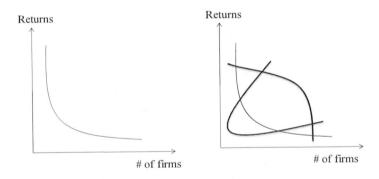

Source: Author's own creation.

Figure 5. Distribution of returns and the number of firms (1) – Manufacturing (left) and Service (right).

These arguments are related to geographical elements, heterogeneity of products, and elasticity of substitution. According to the data on U.S., U.K. and Japanese economy in terms of turnover distribution by firm size (See Figure 6 through Figure 8), the curve shifts in various ways in the service sector. This brings us a question and one hypothesis that the service sector grows because of the profit structure variations by firm size even if the service sector maintains the same productivity level. Behind these variations, it is important to take a look at the trends of capital, labor, and productivity in each country and each service sector so that we can identify structural factors leading to these situations.

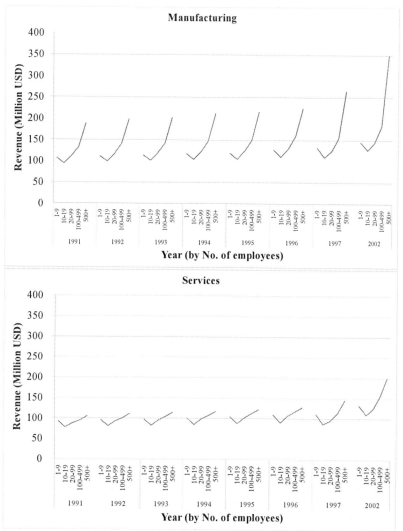

Note: 1) Unit: Turnover (USD million) divided by number of employees. 2) International Standard of Industrial Classifications, Rev. 3, 4-digit level. 3) Years covered: 1991-1997, and 2002 (1997 and 2002 are benchmark years). 4) National Size Class (NSC 1-5) corresponds to 1-9 employees (NSC1), 10-19 (NSC2), 20-99 (NSC3), 100-499 (NSC4), and 500+ (NSC5) respectively. 5) Data on turnover by enterprise size class is taken from OECD instead.

Source: Figures created by author based on data obtained from OECD databases including Structural and Demographic Business Statistics (SDBS) (2008e) [5], Statistics on Enterprises by Size Class (SEC), Structural Statistics for Industry and Services (SSIS) [6], Business Statistics by Size Class (BSC), and Business Demography (BD) [7].

Figure 6. Turnover per employee by size class (US): Manufacturing (Left) and Services (Right).

According to Figure 6 on U.S. economy, the distribution of turnover is gradually shifted to larger firms, and the gap between smaller firms and larger firms are becoming large in manufacturing. The trend in services is different in that the turnover per employee is far larger than that of manufacturing and smaller firms are gaining more profits per employee than manufacturing. At the same time, the bottom of the curves in manufacturing shows that the turnover for smaller firms has not increased over the years. As for services, the curve has shifted upward and downward. Please refer to Figure 7 and Figure 8 for the trend in U.K. and Japan respectively.

---

[5] The first provides information on a number of economic variables broken down by 4-digit International Standard of Industrial Classification Revision 3 (ISIC Rev. 3) industries and is referred to as the Structural Statistics on Industry and Services database (SSIS). The second provides the same industry level of information as the SSIS database but this is also broken down by size classes of businesses, and is referred to as the Business Statistics by Size Class database (BSC) database at http://puck.sourceoecd.org/vl=286302/cl=26/nw=1/rpsv/~6678/v2006n14/s1/p11

[6] The SSIS database contains information relating to the economic activity, including employment, of industries at a very detailed level (International Standard of Industrial Classifications, Revision 3, 4-digit level). Variables include: turnover, value-added, investment, wages and salaries, employees and number of enterprises to name but a few. Monetary variables are typically, although not always, presented in millions of national currency, and employment variables in numbers of persons employed; hours worked are typically expressed in thousands, and number of enterprises/establishments in units. See http://lysander.sourceoecd.org/vl=936377/cl=31/nw=1/rpsv/~4021/v165n1/s7/p1

[7] The BD database contains information relating to business births (often referred to as business entries); business deaths (often referred to as business exits) and business survival rates. These variables are expressed as ratios and percentages, when multiplied by 100.

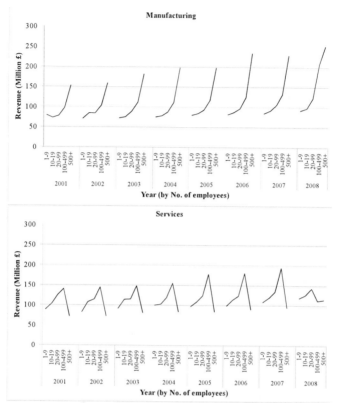

Note: 1) Unit: Turnover[8] (£ million) divided by number of employees[9]. 2) UK Standard Industrial Classification of Economic Activities (SIC) 2003/2007. 3) National Size Class (NSC 1-5) is employed.

Source: Figures created by author based on data obtained from Small and Medium-sized Enterprise (SME) Statistics for the UK and regions (1994-2007)[10].

Figure 7. Turnover per employee by size class (UK): Manufacturing (Left) and Services (Right).

---

[8] Turnover is defined as the value of sales, work done and services rendered. It excludes VAT. Turnover data for registered enterprises is obtained from the Inter-Departmental Business Register (IDBR).

[9] Employment refers to the number of employees plus the number of self-employed people that run the enterprise. Both full-time and part-time employees are counted. Each part-time employee will be counted as one whole employee associated with the enterprise. Therefore, if someone has two part-time jobs, then the person is double counted.

[10] See http://stats.berr.gov.uk/ed/sme/smestats2008-meth.pdf for methodology.

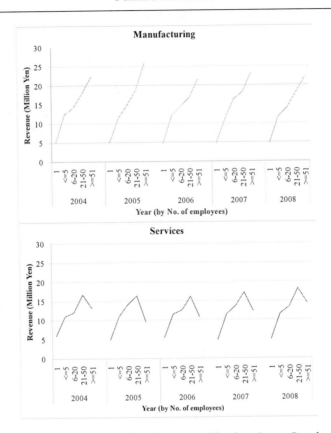

Note: 1) Data period: 2004-2008. 2) Industry classification: Japan Standard Industrial Classification: Construction (E), Manufacturing (F), Information and telecommunication (H), Transportation (I), Wholesale and Retail (I), Real estate (L), Restaurant and lodging (M), and Services (Q). 3) Firm size classes: 1, 2-5, 6-20, 21-50, and +51. 4) Turnover (unit): Million yen.

Source: Figures created by author based on data obtained from Survey of SMEs business activity, The Small and Medium Enterprise Agency of Japan (2004-2008).

Figure 8. Turnover per employee by size class (Japan): Manufacturing (Left) and Services (Right).

According to KLEMS data (National Institute for Economic and Social Research & Groningen Growth and Development Centre, 1970-2008)[11], the

---

[11] 'EU KLEMS' stands for *EU level analysis of capital (K), labour (L), energy (E), materials (M) and service (S) inputs* according to EU KELMS project homepage (http://www.euklems.net/). KLEMS database has information on capital input and its

contribution of IT stock to value-added growth is very strong in U.S. financial sector, with a peak in 1998. In addition, the investment into software is large in this sector compared to the other service sectors. The contribution of non-IT stock is also seen with a peak in 1998, which goes down afterwards. In this sector, labor composition and labor hours by high skill workers also seem to contribute to the growth of the sector. In short, IT stock and human resources have contributed to the growth of both value added and gross output. Smaller firms are earning higher turnover per employee. In this sector, the contribution of non-IT stock to sectoral growth has been substantially strong. Moreover, the labor composition by high skill workers between ages 30-49 has supported the growth of this sector. This labor category contributes to the growth of 'Education' sector as well. As for 'Education' and 'Health and restaurants,' the contribution of IT stock seems to be weak.

In U.K., labor composition and hours worked by high skill workers seem to be influencing the trend more than the other sectors. In addition, the stock of IT and non-IT both contribute to the growth of the sector substantially. The composition of high skill workers is high in 'Education' and 'Real estate, renting and business activities' while medium skill workers are dominant in 'Health and social work.' Looking at KLEMS data from the 1980s through 2008, the contribution of IT stock peaked in 2001, which was slightly later than the peak of U.S. (1998) and U.K. (1999-2000). The growth rate of IT stock is far lower than U.S. and U.K. service sector. As for the stock of ICT, Japan has started accumulating from early 1980s ahead of U.S. and U.K. A distinct characteristic of Japanese service sector is the decrease of contribution of hours worked to value-added growth, which can be seen in all service sectors except for 'Health.' High skill female workers compose a large share in 'Education.'

Factors that are common in all three countries are as follows. (i) There is a decrease in the input of short skill workers in all service sectors. (ii) There is a

contribution to value added and gross output. Stock is divided into Computing equipment (IT), Communications equipment, Software, Transport Equipment, Other Machinery and Equipment, Total Non-residential investment, Residential structures, Other assets, ICT assets, Non-ICT assets, and All assets. Total manufacturing (D) including 'food, beverages and tabacco,' 'textiles,' 'leather and footwear,' 'wood and cork,' 'chemical,' 'rubber, plastics and fuel,' 'other non-metallic mineral,' 'machinery,' 'transport equipment,' and 'recycling.' The service sector is divided into Wholesale and retail trade (G), Hotels and restaurants (H), Transport and storage and communication (I), Finance, intermediation (J), Real estate, renting and business activities (K), Public admin and defense (L), Education (M), Health and social work (N), and Other community, social and personal services (O) (Timmer, et al., 2007).

substantial increase in the input of high skill female workers between ages 30-49. (iii) Multi-factor productivity (MFP) has not grown in any of these countries. The fluctuation gap of productivity is narrowing down in U.S. and U.K., which means that the factor for output growth in the service sector has been shifting to the other factors. (iv) The stock of IT and the hours worked by high skilled workers are substantially increasing in 'Financial intermediaries' and 'business activities.' (v) The stock of communications equipment and other machinery equipment is becoming larger in 'Real estate, renting and business activities' compared to the other sectors. Besides, government regulations on pricing and firm size on certain service sectors must be considered carefully, such as Japan's large-scale retail store law[12] that used to regulate maximum floor space for retail and wholesale stores.

1.3. THE ROLE OF R&D IN SERVICES

The previous section deals with the relationship between output growth and firm size. Another important aspect is the perspective of innovation. Innovation fosters competition and brings new goods and services. As for primary sources of innovation, there are numerous literatures explaining the relationship of firm growth, investment behaviors, and productivity as innovation will improve consumer's welfare and social welfare. The role and impact of R&D have been discussed in relation to innovation in a number of past researches, such as Coe et al. (1995; 2009), Cassiman and Veugelers (Cassiman & Veugelers, 2002; Veugelers & Cassiman, 2005) and Melitz (2003) in terms of cooperation and knowledge spillover, the stock of knowledge and elasticity of substitution, the effect of deregulation and trade liberalization, and the impact on productivity. The appropriate quantification of service value and the measurement of its effect to economic growth are important questions in this regard. As for the value of service, the service sector is becoming more technology- and knowledge-intensive as we see particularly in ICT-related services and financial services. It is an on-going problem to measure the impact of these technologies and knowledge capital (tangibles and intangibles) used to provide such services.

---

[12] Formally known as 'Act on the Measures by Large-Scale Retail Stores for Preservation of Living Environment.' Please refer to http://www.japaneselawtranslation.go.jp/law/ detail_main?vm=&id=1852 for more detail.

The definition of R&D is presented in Frascati Manual (OECD, 1980): 'Research and experimental development (R&D) comprise creative work undertaken on a systematic basis in order to increase the stock of knowledge, including knowledge of man, culture and society, and the use of this stock of knowledge to devise new applications' (Djellal, et al., 2003). Furthermore, the flow of knowledge is an important perspective with regard to the innovation in services. OECD says that it is less clear if the production, delivery and consumption of many services can occur at the same time (OECD, 1992, 2005b). Therefore, the innovation in services is distinguished by the following criteria:

- If the innovation involves new or significantly improved characteristics of the service offered to customers, it is a product innovation.
- If the innovation involves new or significantly improved methods, equipment and/or skills used to perform the service, it is a process innovation.
- If the innovation involves significant improvements in both the characteristics of the service offered and in the methods, equipment and/or skills used to perform the service, it is both a product and a process innovation.

The government of the United Kingdom observed that service sectors draw heavily on suppliers and external partners for seeking expertise (Miles, 2006). The government takes the service sector growth led by trade and inter-regional businesses as a vital factor for current and future economic growth. This strategic direction is related to the assumption that the degree of knowledge expertise and its heterogeneity are vital factors for gaining competitiveness in the global market and the acquisition of knowledge is important for the promotion of service innovation both for large and small firms. Regarding these perspectives, EU has published a series of reports on this subject (European Commission, 2008; Kuusisto, 2008a; Kuusisto, 2008b; Kuusisto & Viljamaa, 2006). To achieve these goals regarding the innovation in service and enhanced value-added services, the following items should be paid attention:

- Education and training of personnel in the social sciences and the humanities in universities and special institutions of higher and post-secondary education.

- Innovation activities defined as all those scientific, technical, commercial and financial steps necessary for the implementation of new or improved products or services and their commercial use.
- Other industrial activities including acquisition of technology, other capital acquisition, and production start-up and marketing for new and improved products.
- Production and related technical activities including distribution of goods and services and the various technical services, together with activities using social science disciplines, such as market research.

Typical R&D activities in the service sector are summarized in Table 1. There are several sources, which explain the characteristics of innovation in service, for example, Barras (1986), Jankowski (2001), Miles (2005, 2007), and Hipp and Grupp (2005). The value of R&D investment can be counted in terms of return in market value (Hall, 2007; Hall, Jaffe, & Trajtenberg, 2001; Hall, Thoma, & Torrisi, 2007). However, there are different possible interpretations in productivity growth among firms if structural aspects are properly controlled, such as physical capital, human capital, firm size, and type of output (Lööf & Heshmati, 2002) as well as government regulations. It is suggested that R&D affects knowledge stock and flow, in a different way from those of manufacturing, leading to an increase in heterogeneity and/or the degree of expertise.

As for the business size dimension, it is suggested that R&D investment is propensity to firm size (to the first approximation) while firm growth is independent of firm size in accordance with Gibrat's law (Gibrat, 1931). These propositions are discussed, for example, in Griliches et al. (Griliches, 1994; Klette & Griliches, 2000), Bayoumi, Coe, and Helpman (1999), Mulkay, Hall and Mairesse (2001), Pagano and Schivardi (2003), and Klette and Kortum (2004). Cohen and Klepper (1996) also describe typical characteristics with regard to the investment size of R&D by enterprises. The first fact is that the likelihood for firms to invest into R&D activities increases with firm size. The second stylized notion is that the likelihood approaches one as the firm size becomes larger.

Table 1. Types of R&D in Services

Type of the service	Typical R&D activities
Finance, insurance, and real estate industries	
Commercial and investment banking, insurance, and commercial and residential real estate industries	Insurance and financial mathematics, IT systems development for the back office and delivery, service scripts development for the front desk personnel
Business services, and legal services	
Legal services, advertising, engineering and architecture, public relations, accounting, R&D, and consulting	Creative design, socio-economic research (market research, technical science, consumer behavior, management research, and media research)
Transportation and communications	
Electronic media, trucking, shipping, railroads, airlines, and local transportation such as buses and taxies	ICT research and development, logistics simulation, technical science, systems management, planning and socio-economic research, management research, cabin service development, marketing and communications research
Wholesale and retail trade	
Intermediaries between producers and consumers, restaurants, personal services, repair and maintenance services	Socio-economic research, economics, consumer behavior, logistics, shop lay-out, logistics, purchasing management, management research, marketing research, systems management, and simulation
Entertainment, hotel, and motels	
Comprise elements of tourism	Socio-economic research, economics, environmental research, consumer behavior, management research and food science
Government services at the transnational, national, and local levels	
Public servants, armed forces, education, health care, police, and fire departments	Economics, politics and policy research, socioeconomic research, security research and development, planning, medical and health research, gerontology, demographics research, and environmental and energy research
Not for profit agencies	
Charities, churches, museums, and private not for profit health care agencies	Socio-economic research, nutritional research, demographics research, religion-oriented research and medical research

Source: The information in the table is directly obtained from Bryson, Daniels, and Warf (2004) and Kuusisto (2008).

However, as Jankowski and others mention, R&D in services is likely to be performed by firms with less employees and smaller R&D budgets compared to manufacturing (European Commission, 2008; Jankowski, 2001; Miles, 2007) because project-based R&D activities engaging part-time personnel are seen in the service sector more than manufacturing (European

Commission, 2008). In addition, a comprehensive evaluation study (Georghiou, 2003) suggests that use of services is highest in technology-oriented innovative small firms. There seem to be several differences from the conventional stylized facts regarding the relationship of firm size, innovation, R&D, and firm growth as we look at some counterfactuals from the behaviors of the service sector.

However, as Jankowski and others mention, R&D in services is likely to be performed by firms with less employees and smaller R&D budgets compared to manufacturing (European Commission, 2008; Jankowski, 2001; Miles, 2007) because project-based R&D activities engaging part-time personnel are seen in the service sector more than manufacturing (European Commission, 2008). In addition, a comprehensive evaluation study (Georghiou, 2003) suggests that use of services is highest in technology-oriented innovative small firms. There seem to be several differences from the conventional stylized facts regarding the relationship of firm size, innovation, R&D, and firm growth as we look at some counterfactuals from the behaviors of the service sector.

In U.S., $1,970 million was invested in 1990 in R&D with regard to professional, scientific, and technical services (which corresponds to North American Industry Classification System (NAICS) sector 54)[13]. The amount increased to $8,167 million in 2004, out of which 14.1% is purchased R&D. According to Eurostat, 43% of Science and Technology jobs in EU 27 countries are in the service sector (Eurostat, 2007). Employment in knowledge-intensive service sectors stands approximately 30% across EU countries in 2008 (Eurostat, 2008)[14]. Although the level of R&D investment into services is still lower than those of manufacturing sectors, the growth rate of R&D in services in general has outpaced that of the entire service sector. As is commonly seen, the investment into R&D in service has started to increase a few years before the real output of service sector has began to pick up.

According to OECD data ((1990-2007), the investment into R&D in services has been made mainly in 'Computer and related activities,' 'Telecommunications,' and 'Research and development' in U.S. In recent years, the amount of investment into 'Other business activities' has increased. Similarly, U.K. has invested heavily in 'Computer and related activities'.

---

[13] The amount of investment consists of NAICS 5417 (Scientific R&D services). Please refer to satellite account at Bureau of Economic Analysis to be found at http://www.bea.gov/scb/pdf/2007/10%20October/1007_rd_tables.pdf.

[14] Last updated Mar 9, 2010. See http://epp.eurostat.ec.europa.eu/tgm/table.do?tab=table&init=1&plugin=1&language=en&pcode=tsc00012

Japan, which has a substantial portion of manufacturing R&D investment particularly in electronics, the investment into R&D in 'Transport, storage and communications,' 'Computer and related activities,' and 'Research and development' consist a large part of R&D in services. As for the characteristics of R&D in services by funding source, U.S. economy has had a substantial increase in enterprise investment into services with a constant allocation of government budget. The ratio of funds from abroad is large in U.K. economy. As for Japan, R&D investment has been made mainly by businesses in both manufacturing and services.

Although the innovation in service should be identified, would it have caused any negative externality to sectoral growth? For instance, when the heterogeneity in information is low, then, the heterogeneity of knowledge and products are usually low. Then, for instance, even less productive firms can enter into market with a low fixed cost to make firms choose to transit from an old technology to new technology to adopt innovation (Helpman, 2006). When the heterogeneity is high, the fixed cost tends to become also high. In the latter case, the catch-up speed to the lead technology should be slow with a given absorptive capacity equipped with a firm. It is supposed that if the heterogeneity should be high in today's networked service economy, even smaller firms must invest more in knowledge (i.e. R&D and skill development) to afford the heterogeneity.

IT stock and skilled workers have promoted the growth of certain service sectors such as IT services and financial services. For the other sectors, in which the stock of IT and labor have failed to contribute to the output growth, it is important to clarify which factor has generated output and value added, either through geographical locality, elasticity of substitution, or heterogeneity of knowledge. For this purpose, it is necessary to discuss the relationship of these factors with the introduction of IT and knowledge creation activities. As previously mentioned, service sectors tend to rely on external sources for expertise knowledge, and SMEs are usually less capable of engaging in R&D than large enterprises although the ratio of R&D spending by smaller firms is larger than that of manufacturing (OECD, 2006, 2008a; Wolfl, 2005). It is important to consider what factors have contributed to lower the cost of adopting heterogeneous knowledge and/or technology, and thus explain a part of dispersed productivity growth.

1.4. THE FUNCTION OF KNOWLEDGE-INTENSIVE SERVICES (KIS)

One of the areas of research that are focused in recent years is the consideration on knowledge-intensive services (KIS) in economic growth models. In 2006, OECD has published a report on KIS (OECD, 2006). According to the report, KIS are defined as 'the production or integration of service activities, undertaken by firms and public sectors in the context of manufacturing or services, in combination with manufactured outputs or as stand-alone services' (p.7)[15,16]. KIS include R&D, management consulting, information and communications services, human resource management and employment services, legal services (including those related to intellectual property rights), accounting, financing, and marketing-related service activities. KIS play a role to strengthen knowledge production activities not

---

[15] KIS includes the following sectors according to Classification of Economic Activities in the European Community (NACE) and International Standard Industrial Classification of all Economic Activities (ISIC): Real estate activities (NACE 70.x/ISIC 70xx), Renting of machinery and equipment without operator and of personal and household goods (NACE 71.x/ISIC 71xx), Computer and related activities (NACE 72.x/ISIC 72xx i.e. Hardware consultancy, Software consultancy and supply, Data processing, and Database activities), Research and development (NACE 73.x/ISIC 73xx i.e. R&D in natural sciences, engineering, social sciences, and humanities), and Other business activities (NACE 74.x/ISIC 74xx i.e. Legal, accounting, book-keeping and auditing activities; Tax consultancy; Market research and public opinion polling; Business and management consultancy; Holdings, architectural and engineering activities and related technical consultancy, Technical testing and analysis, Advertising, and Labour recruitment and provision of personnel).
According to Miles (2005), traditional professional services, which are liable to intensive users of new technology, include marketing, training, design, a part of financial services, office services, building services, management consultancy, accounting and bookkeeping, legal services, and environmental services. On the other hand, new technology-based KIS are such as computer networks and telematics, telecommunications, software, training in new technologies, design involving new technologies, office services involving new office equipment, building services, management consultancy, technical engineering, environmental services involving new technology, and R&D consultancy. In contrast, non-KIS services include services i.e. health and medical services, post, transport and distribution, consumer financial and real estate services, education services, broadcast and other mass media, public administration, repair/maintenance, retail and wholesale, social welfare services, hospitality and catering, leisure and tourism, personal consumer services and entertainment.

[16] Miles (2005) also says that KIS are characterized by the capabilities of providing new types of knowledge input through technologies, regulations and social change, and thus being increasingly internationalized and outsourced as tradable services.

only in service sectors but also in manufacturing. KIS are a type of services to be consumed as final output but also influence the performance of other organizations and value chains beyond sectors by being consumed as intermediaries. Please refer to Appendix C for the analysis on KIS to investigate if KIS would contribute to the growth of productivity.

Finland has transformed its economy into service-dominated market, by focusing on KIS, business services, and trade (Finnish Funding Agency for Technology and Innovation (TeKes), 2007a, 2007c). KIS influence the business performance of organizations and value chains as they contribute to some types of technological and service innovation directly and form a link of technologies and knowledge beyond sectors (OECD, 2006). These services are, as referred to, knowledge-intensive. Some of these services, such as financial services and information services, are also technology intensive. In other words, they are relatively labor intensive, which are generated and delivered by employees with high level of education and specialized expertise knowledge and skills without using production equipment or other types of plant-specific tangible capital. The knowledge capital pertaining to such workers can be firm-specific intangibles. Thus, it is considered that KIS can be an important contributor for economic growth as one of the fastest growing sectors among the other service sectors.

According to OECD (2006), KIS include several functions:

- Renewal service activities – i.e. R&D services and management consulting – are most closely related to innovation
- Routine services – i.e. accounting – contribute to the improvement, maintenance and management of various subsystems within organizations
- Compliance services – i.e. auditing and some legal services – help organizations to work within the legal framework and various regulatory regimes
- Network services – i.e. informal personal networks and professional networks – facilitate communication, knowledge exchange and flexible resource allocation

Kuusisto says that as such KIS focuses on 'service functions and activities' instead of the actors, and that activity perspective is appropriate from policy point of view because it deals with the flow of knowledge within and between the firms, value chains, clusters and regions (European Commission, 2008). The report also says that the division of labor and the volume of knowledge are major drivers of KIS. These knowledge-intensive, or labor-intensive, services generated partly through R&D activities, which are enhanced and innovated furthermore by the use of IT. The most of R&D in services is accounted for business services, post and telecommunications, and computer related services. R&D in IT services has been a public focus in a number of countries. For instance, Sweden has a program called Verket Foer Innovations System (VINNOVA)[17] for developing IT platform to facilitate infrastructure for knowledge management in services. VINNOVA has also programs for small businesses that carry on R&D. This program encompasses: IT support services, services supporting new value chains and knowledge based platform, e-services in public administration, and IT in homecare and elderly care. In some cases, a wide range of services need to be aligned with new generations of IT, and biotechnology (European Commission, 2008). As such, IT works as a tool for creating new services.

A variety of information technologies are being developed to implement innovative services so that the needs of today's economy will be met. Ubiquitous network encompasses web, overlay network, sensor networks, and grid computing with information filtering and search algorithms. There is a collaborative information network such as Cancer Biomedical Informatics Grid[18], which promotes community-based research and communication. The practice and management of R&D is refined where a good match of demand and solution is made through web-based database of solution providers.

IT services have had an important role regarding R&D process and organization. As previously mentioned, R&D activities in services are performed on a project basis in many cases. IT can be used to organize and facilitate R&D undertaken by multidisciplinary business units, teams, and firms. In this sense, skilled staff has an essential role to play for coordinating R&D in services enhanced by the introduction of IT. Publicly-funded R&D is likely to focus on the implementation and improvement of IT-related business environments with the support of educational training for IT skills. IT are used for the support of SMEs as a part of government policy measures. Some European governments support SMEs by implementing service-oriented public infrastructure (Borresen, 2007; Brun & Lanng, 2006; Stauning, 2007). The public infrastructure for SMEs can be designed for lowering barriers to entry to promote their participation in domestic and global market, optimizing business operation and reducing marginal cost and administration costs

---

[17] See http://www.vinnova.se/en/

[18] See https://cabig.nci.nih.gov/

through the shared infrastructure. The other desired functionalities are web-based directory of firms for improved accountability and transparency, promoting peer-to-peer payment mechanisms, activity-based service charge for meeting the needs of customized services, and enhanced interaction between vendor and user as well as external professionals, such as KIS, for harvesting long-tail of service business and creating new services.

These kinds of collaborative and innovative activities contribute to the growth of service sectors, which is common as well as distinctive from manufacturing. IT have a huge impact on innovativeness, adaptability, and quality of service development (NESTA Policy and Research Unit, 2008). Atkinson and Castro (2008) describe a list of benefits, which IT can bring. Among those is the benefit for developing countries. The World Economic Prospect (World Bank, 2008, 2009) articulate that the recent financial turmoil is bringing substantial uncertainty to developing countries due to swings of food and fuel prices, and that demand for commodities is not expected to outstrip supply over the long run.

These new services offer channels for financing and commercialization, and access to education, healthcare, and expertise knowledge for SMEs and people who did not have access to any of those before. To continue to drive such technological innovation and, hence, promote the innovation in service, we may need to focus on the important, dynamic role of SMEs, and facilitate the co-evolutionary process of IT with other technological fields (European Commission, 2008). In today's socio-economic context, innovation in IT holds three-faced importance in relation to services: networking of knowledge and expertise, the promotion of business and trade, and a new solution for the development of global economy through service-oriented infrastructure (Atkinson & Castro, 2008).

For the growth of service economy, Freeman and Soete (2007) express a surprising comment. 'Frontiers and characteristics that were important last century may well no longer be so relevant today and indeed may even be positively misleading…GDP, probably the most widely-used economic indicator in the world, are beset with problems in their measurement, especially now that services account for between 60 to 80 per cent of total output in most developed countries'. In response to such a circumstance, a number of countries and research institutions are challenging the task of establishing innovation performance measurement scheme and policy assessment methodology.

In summary, the growth of services in relation to innovation, R&D activities in services are coordinated and facilitated with the utilization of KIS and IT, giving an impact on knowledge expertise in particular, which can be considered as one of determinants for innovation. Taking this connection of technological and knowledge innovation into consideration, the following section discusses Cobb-Douglas functions for further statistical and empirical research for the service sector.

Chapter 3

PRODUCTIVITY AND INNOVATION IN SERVICE SECTORS

2.1. THEORIES ON FIRM SIZE, R&D, AND INNOVATION

Innovation has been measured generally by productivity (process innovation) and product characteristics (product innovation) in past researches. Suppose innovation is occurring in service sectors, we must be able to identify any improvement of products in terms of characteristics, and/or an addition of new characteristics (Ohashi, 2007). Two major elements which are seen commonly across service sectors are that service sectors draw heavily on suppliers and external sources for expertise (NESTA Policy and Research Unit, 2008), and that the size of firms are likely to be smaller than manufacturing sectors (OECD, 2008a). One possible hypothesis to explain these two conditions is that the relation between firm size and productivity is changing in service sectors with a given increase in the heterogeneity in firms and products. This situation is presumably related to the elasticity of substitution in terms of knowledge expertise.

These phenomena can be understood partly from the nature of networks. When large enterprises had emerged mainly in manufacturing sectors, many individuals were working within large organizations in similar environments. In such a case, generally the multiplicity of individuals' information was said to be reduced. However, after a certain period of time while organizations had faced various situations, the heterogeneity of information pertaining to individuals increased. In addition, as organizations formed connections with each other, the context that gives meaning to the information became more complicated, this caused the multiplicity and heterogeneity of information to increase due to the existence of networks at both enterprise and individual levels. Meanwhile, firms are challenged to develop knowledge to afford the multiplicity and heterogeneity, and achieve profitability. It is proposed that the innovation in service can be captured in the relationship of firm size and turnover given a certain level of heterogeneity in knowledge.

In the context of service economy, it is important to review previous literatures showing the relationship among firm size, profitability, and investment into R&D from the viewpoints of output growth, elasticity of knowledge, other types of co-investments into knowledge (i.e. software and education) to generate or facilitate the creation of knowledge, and productivity improvement in relation to IT infrastructures. It is also suggested that pricing and regulations on service sectors, conversion from flow to stock accounting of R&D investment, and impact of cash flow on R&D investment (particularly from the perspectives of SMEs) should be considered. In the following section, previous literatures are going to be reviewed to clarify the focal points of analysis in panel data models that are going to be discussed and identified in later sections. Theoretical findings are reflected to the panel data models so that the service sectors are analyzed using data obtained from financial and statistical data on a condition that is closer to real situations and from the perspectives of service innovation. The details of financial and statistical data are outlined in this section.

As for the relationship among firm size, R&D investment, and output growth and/or innovation, Mueller (1967) and Mansfield (1968) found in earlier days that R&D investment is related to firm size positively. Dosi (1988) was concerned with the determinants and effects of innovative activities. His paper aims to identify (a) characteristics of innovative process, (b) factors that are positively or negatively facilitate the generation of new processes and new products, and (c) processes to determine the selection of innovations and their effects on industrial structures. The selection depends on the nature of bridging institutions and own institutional factors. There are formal and informal diffusion and externalities regarding innovative activities, which are associated with (a) specific infrastructures, (b) scale economies, (c) complementary technologies, and (d) technical standards. Dosi observes that appropriability of firms is related to (a) patents, (b) secrecy, (c) lead times, (d) costs and time required for duplication, (e) learning-curve effects, and (f) superior sales and service efforts.

Dosi (1988) said that industrial performance is the results of innovative learning by single firms (together with partners and public institutions), diffusion of innovative knowledge and products as well as processes, and selection among firms. As for patenting, Scherer (1983), Pakes and Griliches (1980) and Schwalbach and Zimmermann (1991) revealed that patents are also proportional to firm size. As for the adoption of technology at the frontier, especially in manufacturing, Dunne (1994) found a similar and positive relationship with firm size.

Acs and Audretsch (1988) also argued by using regression models that innovation is positively related to R&D, skilled labor and the ratio of large firms in industries i.e. electronic computing equipment, process control instruments, radio and TV communication equipment, office machinery, and aircraft. Koeller (1995) used data on the share of R&D investment in the amount of sales in 1977 and showed that innovation improved substantially by high R&D intensity especially for small firms. Cohen and Klepper (1996) investigated the impact of R&D in process and product innovation and found that larger firms in general have an advantage in R&D because they are able to apply the outcome of R&D and spread the costs. Their findings assume that process innovation lowers average costs of production, and product innovation improves product features, and thus, the price that consumers are willing to pay can be increased. Parity is observed for new product innovations across firm size, which is also argued by Acs and Audretsch (1988) and Audretsch and Feldman (1996). In this regard, Pagano and Schivardi (2003) leave the same observation based on their analysis using Eurostat data in 1998. They found from regression analysis that R&D intensity is positively affecting the effect of average firm size in the industry on growth.

Fishman and Rob (1999) investigated U.S. manufacturing and retail sectors. Profits of firms become higher if the cost at the beginning of a period is higher than the cost at the end of the period. They categorize firms into classes according to the customers with a certain level of search cost, and assume that R&D expenditures and prices on the customer base rise only firms go across the classes. R&D investment, then, depends on firm's cost cutting efforts in relation to the cost incurred according to the customer base, and so, it is suggested that larger firms invest more into R&D because they can spread the costs over their large size of customer base. This situation leads to a situation where large firms maintain lower marginal costs and prices on average, which generates higher profits.

Klette and Griliches (2000) challendged several stylized facts on R&D and firm size, such as the following: (1) R&D intensities are independent of sales. (2) Firm growth is independent of size. (3) The size distibution of firms is highly skewed with persistent differences in firm sizes. Klett and Kortum (2004) summarized several stylized facts about firm size, productivity and R&D, which goes in the same line with Klette and Griliches (2000). For example, productivity and R&D across firms are positively related, whereas productivity growth is not strongly related to firm's R&D investment. Larger firms are likely to invest into R&D more than small firms, which increases proportionally to sales although the intensity of R&D is heterogeneous and independent of firm size and some firms report zero R&D. In Klett and Kortum (2004), innovative intensity is expressed as a ratio of investment into R&D over stock of knowledge. In their arguments, it is assumed that the number of firms in a cohort decreases over time and the survivors grow bigger on average. The quality of innovation for growth is described according to a version of one product, and the contribution of innovation to utility is obtained from the amount of consumption of any version of the good multiplied by the default quality of the product.

Shefer and Frenkel (2005) examined several determinants which influence R&D expenditure and innovation in addition to firm size, for example, organizational structure, ownership type, industrial branch and location. It is observed that the rate of investment in R&D is not correlated with firm size in industries such as plastics and metals. Cassiman and Veugelers (2002) investigated the role of external information, or incoming spillovers (i.e. publicly available information for innovation such as patent, specialist, conference, meetings, publications, trade shows, and seminars) on firm's decision making as well as appropriability [1] (i.e. ability to appropriate the returns from innovation by legal protection, secrecy, etc.). According to their results of first-step regressions, firm size is significantly related to firm's decision making on building cooperation with other firms at 0.135, incoming spillovers at 0.00514 (not significant), appropriability at -0.0137 (not significant), and permanent R&D at 0.0457 (not significant). They stated that larger firms are more willing to cooperate.

Eaton, Kortum and Kramarz (2009) analyzed the relationship of output and firm size based on Eaton and Kortum (2002) and Bernard, Eaton, Jensen, and Kortum (2003) although R&D is not explicitly included in their model. The market is divided across N geography separated areas in selling a product (the continuums of goods, J). Goods produced in country i with efficiency

---

[1] Cassiman and Veugelers (2002) mention that lower appropriability increases a chance for free ride on other firms' R&D investment.

greater than z is $J\{1-\exp[-(T_i / J)z^{-\theta}]\}$. Each location is characterized by such as the measure of ideas T_i, or the average efficiency in the country, the input cost ω_i, and the component of the entry barrier for goods. To sell in market, a firm must sell equal to or more than σE_n, in which E is goods and σ is the heterogeneity in preferences. It is important to note that mean sales are expressed as $\bar{x}_n = \dfrac{\sigma E_n}{1-1/\theta}$, which shows that the sales distribution is Pareto with slope θ.

Tsai and Wang (2005) investigated Taiwanese manufacturing companies on the Taiwan Stock Exchange. They used a fixed effect model and random effect model to find hat R&D productivity is higher for both large firms and small firms, and thus, small firms can gain benefits from developing new products. It is also suggestive that R&D and market development activities i.e. marketing are complementary. In this study, Tsai and Wang (2005) investigated R&D in terms of elasticity of output, which is the percentage change in TFP divided by the percentage change in the growth rate of R&D capital. Firm size is treated as a moderator variable. The growth rate of TFP (*f*) is derived from $f_{it} = a_{it} + \gamma r_{it} + \varepsilon_{it}$, in which r is growth rate of R&D capital and γ is elasticity of R&D capital ($\gamma = \beta_0 + \beta_1 S + \beta_2 S^2$ with S as firm size). This function can be rewritten as $f_{it} = a_{it} + \beta_0 r_{it} + \beta_1 r_{it} S_{it} + \beta_2 r_{it} S_{it}^2 + v_{it}$ with R&D output elasticity (β_0), the impact of firm size (β_1), and change in the impact of firm size on the elasticity (β_2).

Table 2. Determinants on R&D Cooperation

Paper	Partner type	Major significant determinants	Sample	Econometric model
Bayona, Garcia-Marco, and Huerta (2001)	All types of firms	Firm (size[+], R&D intensity[+]), Industry	1652 Spanish firms (SMEs and large firms)	Logit
Belderbos, Carree, Diederen, Lokshin, and Veugelers (2004)	Competitor, customer, supplier, university, public research institute. All types of firms	Firm (size[+], R&D intensity[+], incoming spillover), Industry	2194 Dutch firms (European Community Innovation Survey)	Multivariate probit
Colombo and Grilli (2005)	All types of firms	Firm (size[+], patent[+], venture capital financing), Founder, Industry	522 Italian firms (startups)	Hazard, panel probit
Fontana, Geuna, and Matt (2006)	University, public research institute	Firm (size[+], R&D intensity[+], patent[+], subsidy or public support[+]), Industry, Country	558 EU firms (SMEs)	Negative binominal
Fritsch and Lukas (2001)	Competitor, customer, supplier, public research institute	Firm (size[+], R&D intensity[+]), Industry, Region	1800 German firms	Two-stage model with logit
López (2008)	All types of firms	Firm (size[+], R&D intensity[+], subsidy or public support[+]), Industry	6026 Spanish firms	Simultaneous equations
Miotti and Sachwald (2003)	Vertical, competitor, university, public research institute	Firm (size[+], R&D intensity[+], incoming spillover[+], cost and risk[+]), Industry	2378 French firms	Logit

Table 2. (Continued)

Paper	Partner type	Major significant determinants	Sample	Econometric model
Mohnen and Hoareau (2003)	University, public research institute	Firm (size[+], R&D intensity[+], patent[+], group affiliation[+], subsidy or public support[+]), Industry, Country	9191 French, German, Irish and Spanish firms	Trivariate probit
Motohashi (2005)	University	Firm (size[+], R&D intensity[+], patent[+]), Industry	724 Japanese firms	Binary choice
Tether (2002)	Competitor, customer, supplier, public research institute, consultant	Firm (size[+], R&D intensity[+]), Industry	1275 UK firms	Logit
Veugelers and Cassiman (2005)	University	Firm (size[+]), Industry	325 Belgian firms	Instrumental variable (IV) probit

Source: Information on the table is directly obtained in Okamuro, Honjo and Kato (2009). There are minor modifications by the author.

Lotti, Santarelli, and Vivarelli (2009) investigated radio, TV, and communication equipment industry in Italy to test if Gibrat's law is accepted (please be noted that the role of R&D is not considered). The main argument is the relation between firm size and growth rate. It is found that Gibrat's law is rejected *ex ante,* and firm age and growth is inversely related. Besanko and Doraszelski (2004) applied Markov-perfect equilibriums and found that under price competition, the industry is likely to diverge into a large firm and one small firm with the depreciation of investment is positive. They also found that under quantity competition, the size of firms tend to become homogenous. They suggested that their models could be extended to investigate the impact on product differentiation. Please refer to the following table for the other past researches on R&D investment behaviors and cooperation in relation to firm size.

As for knowledge spillovers, Bayoumi, Coe and Helpman (1999) relate total factor productivity (TFP) to R&D investment and trade although they did not include firm size in their analysis. They hold the ratio of R&D expenditures to GDP constant. R&D investment is considered to give an indirect impact on output through capital accumulation, and direct impact on output through TFP. The effect of trade is expressed in learning from trade partners, and an increased variety of intermediate goods. In their model, TFP is determined endogenously by R&D capital[1], international R&D spillovers[2], and trade. Future increases in TFP are translated into an increase in current investment. They found that R&D investment can contribute greatly to the domestic GDP and of other countries. The outcome of R&D is expressed in the improvement of efficiency assuming constant marginal costs (Ericson & Pakes, 1995).

Sargent and Williams (2005) examined surplus appropriability, knowledge spillovers, creative destruction, and duplication externalities. Consumer surplus is generally not perfectly appropriated to future investment, and the situation, referred to 'underinvestment,' may lead to knowledge spillover problem. They assumed an elasticity of substitution between capital goods, and suggested that only a part of innovative firms increases the variety of intermediate goods, and the rest only upgrade existing intermediate goods. They define R&D as the search for new designs for intermediate goods, and

---

[1] R&D capital is an accumulation of R&D investment plus depreciation.

[2] International R&D spillovers correspond to the effect of foreign R&D investment via import share.

suppose that there is a constant return to R&D investment, which is derived from current market value of the new design.

Acemoglu, Aghion, Lelarge, Van Reenen, and Zilibotti (2007) addressed the problem of technological frontiers who are able to generate new technologies with limited information. In this case, the distance to the frontier technology is derived from the gap between a firm's productivity and the highest productivity in the industry. The issue of the distance from the frontier is also addressed in Griffith, Redding and Van Reenen (2003). They examined R&D-based absorptive capacity, which is defined as the relative level of TFP defined as ln(TFP in frontier countries)-ln(TFP in non-frontier conutry), and that of multiplied by the number of employees engaging in R&D. Efficiency term (A) is denoted as either productivity or the quality of intermediate goods:

$$E_{t-1}\ln\left(\frac{A_{i1t}}{A_{i1t-1}}\right) = \lambda_i \hat{H}_{it-1}^R \ln\gamma + \mu_i \ln\left(\frac{A_{F1t-1}}{A_{i1t-1}}\right) + \lambda_i \hat{H}_{it-1}^R \phi_i \ln\left(\frac{A_{F1t-1}}{A_{i1t-1}}\right)$$

with expectation (E), the size of innovations (γ), the pace of autonomous technology transfer (μ), the probability of research success (λ), absorptive capacity of technology transfer, equilibrium research employment (H), and frontier country (F). According to the result, the absorptive capacity is positively impacting the growth of productivity.

Aw, Roberts and Xu (2008) investigated the relationship between export and R&D investment. They used a Markov process to estimate a firm's productivity in relation to R&D activity. Productivity (ω) is expressed in:

$$\omega_{it} = g(\omega_{it-1}, d_{it-1}, e_{it-1}) + \xi_{it}$$
$$= \alpha_0 + \alpha_1\omega_{it-1} + \alpha_2(\omega_{it-1})^2 + \alpha_3(\omega_{it-1})^3 + \alpha_4 d_{it-1} + \alpha_5 e_{it-1} + \alpha_6 d_{it-1}e_{it-1} + \xi_{it}$$

d_{it-1} is firm's R&D investment, and e_{it-1} is export market participation in the previous period. Productivity improvement in stochastic nature is ξ, and expected increase in productivity is represented in α. It is found that a firm with a given productivity level, the firm is more likely to continue to invest into R&D and to export. However, R&D investment generates little impact on the return to exporting.

As for the impact on R&D, which turns into the behavior of productivity, Mulkay, Hall and Mairesse (2001) incorporated the impact of output and cash flow [3] on the amount of investment. They used Generalized Method of Moments (GMM) to find that the output-capital gap is closed at a faster rate for ordinary capital and a slower rate for R&D investment in response to sales growth. The profit growth affects future investment pattern, which is observed in a lag of one year in their estimation. Standard deviation of sales growth and distribution of productivity are used to represent the heterogeneity, and the distance from the frontier technology is also expressed as the gap between the productivity of a firm and the highest productivity in the same industry.

Bloom (2007) investigated how uncertainty gives impact on R&D investment as an issue of adjustment costs. It is mentioned that normally time constant uncertainty is assumed in order to derive analytical solutions, and the adjustment costs of changing knowledge stocks incurs due to a change in the rates of change of its stock (R&D). They found that higher uncertainty reduces the responsiveness to sales growth and increases the responsiveness to lagged R&D expenditure. Bloom (2007) assumes that R&D depreciates over time. Thus, the uncertainly increases temporarily, R&D will be reduced at the steady state.

It is supposed that all of these issues regarding R&D are related to the depreciation of R&D capital in one way or the other. Hall (2007) discussed the measurement method in detail [4]. For a certain level of capital stock (K) and R&D investment (R), it is described as $K_{it} = (1-\delta)K_{i,t-1} + R_{it}$. Then, the output elasticity (γ) of knowledge or intangible capital (K) with respect to the output elasticity (β) of tangible capital (A) is $\gamma / \beta = c_K^* K / c_A A$ with cost of capital (c). According to market value approach, the depreciation of R&D is derived based on

$$(\hat{\gamma}_t / \hat{\alpha}_t) * [(p_{it}^R K_{it}) / (p_{it}^I A_{it})] = (1-\delta_R / 1-\delta_I) * [(p_{it}^R K_{it}) / (p_{it}^I A_{it})]$$

with the overall market movements in Tobin's Q denoted as α, in which R and I correspond to R&D and tangible capital respectively. The problem of depreciation for R&D, both scientific and non-scientific, is discussed by Corrado, Hulten, and Sichel (2009). They reviewed previous literatures and empirics to estimate R&D depreciation rates as Table 3.

---

[3] The ratio of cash flow is derived from net profits plus depreciation to the beginning of period capital stock.

[4] Hall mentions that data are suggesting appreciation rather than depreciation of R&D capital over the period.

Table 3. Depreciation Rates[5]

Category Depreciation Rate	%
Computerized information (other than software)	33
R&D, scientific	20
R&D, non-scientific	20
Brand equity	60
Firm-specific resources	40

Note: According to Corrado, Hulten, and Sichel (2009), 1) The depreciation rate for computerized information is taken from U.S. Bureau of Economic Analysis (five-year service life). 2) According to Bernstein and Mamuneas (2006), the depreciation rate is found to be 18% for U.S. Ishaq and Prucha (1996) presented a rate of 12%. Pakes and Schankerman (1979) obtained 25% for Europe. Pakes and Schankerman (1986) suggested a range of 11–26%.

Source: Contributions are obtained from Corrado, Hulten, and Sichel (2009).

2.2. CONSTRUCTION OF MODELS-PANEL DATA ANALYSES

In most literatures that are reviewed in the previous section, data from manufacturing industries are used for constructing the models. In addition, firm's capacity for innovation is not often addressed in a way which shows firm's competence to use external sources for expertise in the innovation in service, and to introduce IT for supporting their uses. Several reports published by EU say that system competent providers may have an important function in lowering the threshold for small firms, and the first experience of using external KIS[6] can have far-reaching effects on the firm's future service use (EU Scientific and Technical Research Committee, 2008; European Commission, 2008, 2009). One of the reports mentions also that from the policy perspective, the system competence as a prerequisite of public sector funding is not purely a negative phenomenon (Kuusisto, 2008a). It is true when public policy deals with projects such as e-invoicing for SMEs (Brun &

---

[5] In this chapter, the depreciation of R&D is taken from this table for the panel data analyses.

[6] There is an empirical analysis on KIS using French micro-data. Please refer to Lelarge (2009).

Lanng, 2006). Public infrastructure is being provided to support SMEs business operation, participation into public procurement, and reduce administrative burdens.

According to the above-mentioned reports, system competence can be a proxy for innovation potential, and more research are required to clarify the relationship of such system competence and growth potentials. This aspect is surveyed in Europe in 2009 (Eurostat, 1992-2009) so that the relationship with service differentiation (technical knowledge), productivity and service enhancement, all of which are related to value-added services, is analyzed. The survey intends to address the role of KIS providers for SMEs that represent potential users of expertise knowledge, because the use of KIS may suffice a limited use of financial, human and educational resources in SMEs, and as a source of external expertise, they may cover their lower system competence. In this sense, it is important to investigate the use of networks and IT infrastructure by SMEs.

To analyze the abovementioned conditions, this chapter argues macro-micro models, which consist of two sets of methodology: macro and micro panel data models. The macro-micro techniques combine macro and micro modeling with different degrees of integration (Bourguignon & Pereira da Silva, 2003). According to Zellner (2008), sectoral disaggregation and its modeling will be used much more in the future econometrics. The current level of imprecision in econometric analysis and forecast is caused by the lack of industry-level analysis involving the investigation on sectoral demands for factors, output supply, profit shocks, innovations, etc., which are often not observed directly in macroeconomic analysis. Zellner (2008) summarizes that the introduction of firm entry-exit relation in each product market model enables us to observe nonlinear and co-integrated effects in individual and multiple sectors from macroeconomic viewpoints with higher accuracy.

This approach allows us to evaluate micro-level effects of macroeconomic impacts. From macroeconomic perspectives, we need equations to build structural models with some assumptions i.e. utility-maximizing consumer under a budget constraint with tax-benefit system via public IT infrastructure. After structural parameters are estimated in macroeconomic models, results are imputed into micro models (top-down) or vice versa (bottom-up). In this research, the analyses employ the bottom-up approach. Micro models are useful for the assessment of heterogeneous population, product characteristics, and firms. These models clarify a mechanism by which individuals and firms are allocated to a policy or market conditions. The heterogeneity stems from differences in demand patterns and socio-economic characteristics, and is observed in source data and exogenous factors (Essama-Nssah, 2007). The following sections will present micro and macroeconomic models in detail.

2.3. DYNAMIC MICRO MODELS

Dynamic panel data models are used when a large amount of cross-section data are available while time-series data are relatively short, in which *lagged* dependent *variables* appear in correlation with error term. Arellano et al. (1989; 2001), Hahn, Hausman, and Kuersteinerm (2002), Pakes and Ericson (1998), Pakes (2003), Ackerberg, et al. (2007) and many others have approached to these issues using instrument variables (IV). Data on public infrastructure have not been accumulated as a historical data over several decades, and the correlation with economic growth is yet to be confirmed. Therefore, this chapter focuses on structural parameters and the role of intermediate inputs to control productivity as well as imperfect instrument variables (IIV) based on Olley and Pakes (1996) and Ackerberg et al. (2007) incorporating the findings of Levinsohn and Petrin (2003), Bajari, Benkard, and Levin (2007), Andrews and Stock (2007), and Nevo and Rosen (2008).

Production Functions

First of all, the following Cobb-Douglas production function is defined for a firm j:

$$Y_j = A_j^{\beta_a} K_j^{\beta_k} L_j^{\beta_l} \qquad\qquad (2.3.1)$$

where output (Y_j) is a function of capital (K_j) and labor (L_j) with (unobserved) Hicksian neutral efficiency level of the firm (A_j). By taking the natural logarithmic of the equation, the following equation is derived:

$$y_{jt} = \beta_0 + \beta_k k_{jt} + \beta_a a_{jt} + \beta_l \ell_{jt} + \varepsilon_{jt} + \eta_{jt} \qquad\qquad (2.3.2)$$

Based on Olley and Pakes (1996) and Ackerberg et al. (2007), β_0 is defined as the mean efficiency level across firms. ε_{jt} and η_{jt} represent knowledge networks and the deviation from the mean respectively. Knowledge network represents a composite effect of any efforts for facilitating knowledge creation, and sharing and spillovers particularly seen in the service sector. When they are caused by known factors, the choice of labor for firm j is:

$$L_j = \left[\frac{p_j}{w_j} \beta_l e^{\beta_0 + \omega_j} K_j^{\beta_k} \right]^{\frac{1}{1-\beta_l}}$$

(2.3.3)

with price of output (p_j), wage (w_j), and ω_i as a set of parameters $(\varepsilon_{jt}, \tau_{it}, \eta_{jt})$. Unobserved productivity (ω_{jt}) takes a form of the following function:

$$F(\omega_{jt+1} \mid \{\omega_{j\tau}\}_{\tau=0}^t, l_{jt}) = F(\omega_{jt+1} \mid \omega_{jt})$$

(2.3.4)

where I_{jt} is the firm's information set at time t, and the equation follows an exogenous first order Markov process. Then, the capital accumulation of firm j is assumed to be:

$$k_{jt} = (1 - \delta_T) k_{Tjt-1} + (1 - \delta_I) k_{Ijt-1} + (1 - \delta_{rd}) rd_{jt-1} + i_{jt-1}$$

(2.3.5)

The investment into tangibles may shift more towards the investment into intangibles so that the firm would accumulate knowledge capital to build up expertise by utilizing skilled labor. To observe the investment behavior, the equation above categorizes tangibles (K_{Tj}), intangibles (K_{Ij}), and R&D expenditures with separate depreciation rates (δ_T, δ_I, and δ_{rd}) respectively. i_j denotes investment. The firm's profit at time t is:

$$\pi(k_{jt}, a_{jt}, \ell_{jt}, \omega_{jt}, \Delta_t) - c(i_{jt}, \Delta_t)$$

(2.3.6)

in which Δ_t captures the economic environment surrounding the firm (market size and competition toughness), and $c(\cdot)$ is the cost of investment function. The firm's maximization problem is, then, written as a Bellman equation:

$$V(k_{jt}, a_{jt}, \ell_{jt}, \omega_{jt}, \Delta_t)$$
$$= \max \left\{ \begin{array}{l} \phi(k_{jt}, a_{jt}, \ell_{jt}, \omega_{jt}, \Delta_t), \max_{i_{jt} \geq 0} \{k_{jt}, a_{jt}, \ell_{jt}, \omega_{jt}, \Delta_t\} \\ -c(i_{jt}, \Delta_t) + \beta E[V(k_{jt+1}, a_{jt+1}, \ell_{jt+1}, \omega_{jt+1}, \Delta_{t+1}) \\ | k_{jt}, a_{jt}, \ell_{jt+1}, \omega_{jt}, \Delta_t, i_{jt}] \} \end{array} \right\} \qquad (2.3.7)$$

with the given single-point profit condition in $(\pi \cdot c)$, and the sell-off value of production equipment or service delivery equipment (ϕ). The investment demand function is:

$$i_{jt} = i(k_{jt}, a_{jt}, \ell_{jt}, \omega_{jt}, \Delta_t) = i(k_{jt}, a_{jt}, \ell_{jt}, \omega_{jt}) \qquad (2.3.8)$$

The demand for products in the entire industry is obtained from the distribution of (z_i, v_i). Marginal cost (mc) is log linear with observables ($r_{k,j}$) and productivity (ω_j), which is assumed to be:

$$\ln mc_j = \sum r_{k,j} \theta_k^c + \omega_j \qquad (2.3.9)$$

where r includes the product characteristics (referring to $\tilde{x}_{jt}$ and ξ_{jt} in Equation (2.3.10) in the following subsection), input prices, and the quantity produced. θ is a vector of parameters, and the superscript "c" refers to the interactions of the product characteristic coefficients with total cost.

Demand functions should be defined according to the type of product and industry sector of the firm. The utility of consumer i for product j at time t, which is produced or delivered by a SME, is written as:

$$u_{ijt} = U(\tilde{x}_{jt}, \xi_{jt}, z_{it}, v_{it}, y_{it,0} + y_{it,p} - p_{jt}, \theta) \qquad (2.3.10)$$

where $\tilde{x}_{jt}$ is a K-dimensional vector of observed product characteristics other than price, ξ_{jt} represents unobserved product characteristics, z_{it} is a vector of observed differences in consumer tastes, and v_{it} is a vector of unobserved differences in consumer tastes, and p_{jt} is the price. Note that the consumer's income, y_{it}, can be directly impacted if a member of the household utilizes public infrastructure, is allocated to a certain program, or receives any benefits shared as public goods. The potential amount of increase or decrease in income for such a consumer is denoted as $y_{it,p}$, and thus $y_{it,p}$ becomes 0 if the consumer has not been benefited.

According to Ackerberg et al. (2007), utility depends on the money available to spend outside of this market ($y_{it,0} + y_{it,p} - p_{it}$). When consumer does not choose to purchase the product, the utility of outside good takes the following form:

$$u_{i0} = U(\tilde{x}_0, \xi_0, z_i, v_i, y_{i,0} + y_{i,p} - p_0, \theta) \tag{2.3.11}$$

with $\tilde{x}_0$ as a vector of characteristics of the outside good. Combining (2.3.10) and (2.3.11) makes the total market demand. When u_{ijt} is higher than the utility of any other product, the product j is chosen.

The Role of Trade

According to Kasahara and Lapham (2008) and Kasahara and Rodrigue (2008), foreign intermediates increase productivity at firm level. However, in general, due to the presence of fixed costs and sunk cost for trade, only productive firms are able to decide on entry into trade (less productive firms will need to exit). Productivity gains will lead to increasing import of intermediaries, which will allow some importers to export and let resources be reallocated in terms of volume.

When the market is open, the firm's maximization problem is rewritten in the following equation (Kasahara et al., 2008):

$$V(k_{jt}, a_{jt}, \ell_{jt}, \omega_{jt}, \Delta_t)$$

$$= \max \left\{ \begin{array}{l} \phi(k_{jt}, a_{jt}, \ell_{jt}, \omega_{jt}, \Delta_t), \max_{i_{jt} \geq 0} \{k_{jt}, a_{jt}, \ell_{jt}, \omega_{jt}, \Delta_t\} \\ -c(i_{jt}, \Delta_t) - \Gamma(d_{t-1}, d_t) + \beta E[V(k_{jt+1}, a_{jt+1}, \ell_{jt+1}, \omega_{jt+1}, \Delta_{t+1}) \\ \mid k_{jt}, a_{jt}, \ell_{jt+1}, \omega_{jt}, \Delta_t, i_{jt}]\} \end{array} \right\} \quad (2.3.12)$$

in which $\Gamma(d_{t-1}, d_t)$ is the fixed cost of importing materials and the sunk start-up cost. A firm's discrete choice to import from abroad is denoted by d_{it}, and then it is written as:

$$y_{jt} = \beta_0 + \beta_k k_{jt} + \beta_a a_{jt} + \beta_l \ell_{jt} + \beta_d d_{jt} + \varepsilon_{jt} + \eta_{jt} \quad (2.3.13)$$

Then, the firm's profit condition becomes:

$$\pi(k_{jt}, a_{jt}, \ell_{jt}, \omega_{jt}, \Delta_t) - c(i_{jt}, d_{jt}, \Delta_t) \quad (2.3.14)$$

Decomposing Productivity

Service sectors tend to rely on external sources for expertise, and SMEs are generally less capable of engaging in R&D than large enterprises due to the shortage of funds and skilled workers (OECD, 2006, 2008a; Wolfl, 2005). Therefore, it is important to observe how knowledge is gained and produced by firms in all sizes after they start utilizing IT, using an internal or external source, and/or gaining knowledge as knowledge spillover. Based on NISTEP (2008, 2009), the growth rate of total factor productivity (TFP) takes the following form:

$$\dot{\omega} = \mu + \rho_i \left(\frac{I_j}{Y_j} \right) + \rho_e \left(\frac{E_j}{Y_j} \right) + \rho_s \left(\frac{S_j}{Y_j} \right) + \gamma_j \quad (2.3.15)$$

in which the amount of investment into knowledge (i.e. R&D) is I, and the amount of knowledge purchased from external source (i.e. consultant) is E and the intra-industry knowledge spillover is S^7. Each ρ denotes a firm-specific factor to improve efficiency in knowledge production and transfer.

Productivity (ω_{jt}) in Equation (2.3.4) is defined as a composite effect of ε_{it} and η_{it} determined based on the information that the firm has at time t. To derive the productivity from actual datasets, we have Equation (2.3.15), which encompasses both internal and external efficiency terms to produce knowledge and transfer. This equation is based on the assumption that knowledge is a primary source of innovation, which boosts up productivity in various service sectors.

Now we need to decompose productivity[8] into a set of ε_{it} and η_{it}. To estimate ε_{it}, we have:

$$\omega_{it} = h_{it}(\upsilon_{it}, k_{it}) \tag{2.3.16}$$

with the given amount of KIS (υ_{it}) and a conversion parameter (h). KIS are often used as intermediaries to facilitate intra- and inter-industry knowledge production and transfer (OECD, 2006). KIS are related to all three variables (I, E, and S) in Equation (2.3.15). KIS tend to grow nearly at the same rate of output growth and productivity growth.

In particular, SMEs are now facing the needs of developing expertise knowledge to compete in both domestic and foreign market, and offering services to meet the demand of fragmented services. The degree of specialty and customization makes their products less substitutable with the other products. In such circumstances, this explanation helps us to clarify the mechanism and effect of a small change of fixed and variable costs reduced by employing IT with regard to the dispersion of productivity as well as the product substitutability in the context of a global equilibrium for both incumbent and existing SMEs. To verify the impact empirically, the data on firm sizes can be used directly to observe the changes in productivity.

---

[7] In this chapter, S is approximated by taking standard deviation of the number of firms (head office) and their subsidiaries, and then finding the quantiles of the variables against the quantiles of chi-squared distribution of firms and subsidiaries.

[8] Data can be also obtained from 'productivity' in JSBRI surveys.

2.4. DYNAMIC MACRO MODELS

This chapter follows Canova (2007) to model heterogeneous macro panels. First, GDP is defined as an aggregate of output (Y) for country n:

$$Y_{nt} = A_{nt} L_{nt}^{\alpha} K_{nt}^{1-\alpha}. \qquad (2.4.1)$$

Intermediate goods from firms are used as aggregate intermediate inputs for domestic and foreign markets:

$$\int_0^1 Y_{nt}(i)di = y_t^d + y_t^{\infty} \qquad (2.4.2)$$

with intermediaries for domestic market (y_t^d) and for foreign markets (y_t^{∞}). Intermediaries are used to produce final goods for consumption or investment into capital. Then we have a maximization problem for country n with a given world interest rate with the constraint of:

$$\begin{aligned} & C_{nt} + K_{nt+1} + L_{nt} + sa_{nt+1} \\ & \leq \varsigma_{nt}^{\rho'} K_{nt} L_{nt} + (1-\delta_K) K_{nt} + L_{nt} + (1+r_t) sa_{nt} \end{aligned} \qquad (2.4.3)$$

in which sa_{it} is lending to and/or borrowing from the world, r_t is the rate of lending/borrowing, ς_t^{η} is productivity including the efficiency term $\rho(\rho_i, \rho_e, \rho_s)$ adjusted by Pareto distribution in the global equilibrium (ρ_n'). For capital accumulation, we have

$$1 + r_t = (1 - \delta_K) + \rho_n' GDP_{nt} / K_{nt} \qquad (2.4.4)$$

letting the depreciation rate δ_K to be a weighted average of δ_T and δ_I, and the efficiency term for capital, η_k. Based on Canova (2007), the following two equations are derived with regard to the maximization of utility:

$$L_{nt+1} = (1 - \rho_n')\varsigma_{nt}^* L_{nt}^{\rho^*} + L_{nt} - C_{nt} \tag{2.4.5}$$

$$C_{nt}^{-\varphi} = \beta E_t \left\{ C_{nt+1}^{-\varphi} \left[\rho_n^* \varsigma_{nt+1}^* L_{nt+1}^{\rho^*-1} + (1 - \delta_L) \right] \right\} \tag{2.4.6}$$

letting $\rho^* = \dfrac{\rho' - \rho_n'}{1 - \rho_n'}$. φ is a parameter subject to resource constraint.

Then, we have the following equation to estimate the effect of ICT investment and/or service intermediate inputs (x_i) at time t:

$$y_{nt} = a_{n1}(\ell)y_{nt-1} + a_{n2}(\ell)x_{nt} + \vartheta_n + \eta_{nt} \tag{2.4.7}$$

The long-run effect of x_{it} on y_{it} is derived as a function of $m(\cdot)$:

$$m_1(a_n) = E(1 - a_{n1}(1))^{-1} a_{n2}(1) \tag{2.4.8}$$

Chapter 4

EMPIRICAL ANALYSES

3.1. METHODOLOGY AND DATA[1]

To perform these two types of analyses for selected non-manufacturing sectors in addition to one manufacturing sector by using Japan's firm-level financial data and macro economic data, the following points are emphasized and elaborated in the formulation of regression models. The three manufacturing sectors are analyzed so that a good comparison can be made against the analysis for the service sectors.

The list of sectors to be studied is summarized in Table 4. In this section, the details of data and variables are explained[2]. All regression models are tested by variance inflation factor (VIF) and residual plots, which graphs a residual versus fitted values. Outliers are removed if the value exceeds mean plus standard deviation multiplied by five[3]. As for the firm-level analysis, the first procedure is to perform regression in stepwise method (robust) with 1% (0.01) significance level for removing variables from the model. Dependent variable is revenue and independent variables are *capital (tangibles)*, *capital (intangibles)*, *employee*, and *age*, which are all in logarithmic form. The variables are programmatically removed when collinearity is observed. As a

---

[1] In this section, independent variables for the firm-level analyses are shown in *italic*. To avoid confusion, dependent variable or variables used in the macroeconomic analysis are not in italic except for notations in brakets.

[2] STATA ver.11 is used to perform all test procedures.

[3] In a standard procedure, outliers are removed if it is more than the standard deviation multiplied by three. The author tried this procedure, and still found explicit outliers based on the residual plots. Therefore, the author removed values if it is more than the standard deviation multiplied by five.

supplementary procedure, regression analysis is performed particularly to test interactions of each variable in the previous regression model. The same regression is conducted as the second procedure with an additional variable such as *trade* for firms engaging in trade and *patent* for firms performing R&D. The third procedure is regression performed to take the impact of firm size class into account. The size class is defined based on *National Size Class (NSC)*.

In the fourth procedure, the regression model estimates the production function in the presence of selection bias and simultaneity by using the three-stage algorithm described in Olley and Pakes (1996)[4]. Dependent variable is revenue. As for independent variables, *exit* indicates firm's exit from the market. State variables are appearing in production function such as *age* and *employee*. Proxy variable for unobserved productivity is *KIS*. Free variable used in the second stage only is *patent*. If firms are performing R&D, free variables also include *R&D*. Additional variables used in both the first and second stages are *capital (tangibles)* and *capital (intangibles)*. Bootstrap is set random-number seed to 1 performing 250 bootstrap replications with 99% confidence level. The fifth procedure estimates production functions using intermediate inputs to control for unobservable productivity shocks (Levinsohn & Petrin, 2003)[5]. As for independent variables, *employee* and *age* are used as variables specifying the free variable inputs. Proxy variable specifying intermediate inputs is *KIS*. Capital variable is the total of *capital (tangibles)* and *capital (intangibles)*, which is denoted as *capita (total)*. This procedure is specifically performed to test the impact of intermediate inputs, therefore, the impact of *capital (intangibles)* and *software* are taken into account. The generalized method of moments (GMM) estimator will be used for a grid search to minimize the criterion function[6]. When the data on *KIS* is not sufficient for the regression, instrumental variables[7] are incorporated in place with two-step GMM estimator. In this regression, instrumental variables

---

[4] The detailed description of this command can be found in st0145/opreg.hlp in STATA help file. This file is downloadable and readable online for non-STATA users. Please also refer to Yasar (2008) for the details on how to use this command.

[5] The detailed description of this command can be found in st0060/levpet.hlp in STATA help file.

[6] Please refer to Baum, Schaffer, and Stillman (2003) for the issue regarding the use of instrumental variables (IV) estimation and the generalized method of moments (GMM). This chapter discusses test procedures for heteroskedasticity, overidentification, and endogeneity when IV is used in estimation.

[7] The detailed description of this command can be found in st0030_2/ivreg2.hlp in STATA help file.

are *software* and *KIS*. The other endogenous parameters are *capital (tangibles)*, *capital (intangibles)*, and *employee*. As an option, fixed effect is also studied with Hausman test. In this case, *employee²* and *age²* are also incorporated. In the procedures in which *NSC* is included as dummies, *employee²* and *age²* are introduced into the analyses. These variables are useful for the observation on the speed of change and its scale.

Following the firm-level analysis, productivity is estimated in terms of capital and labor productivity. After importing datasets from the previous firm-level analysis, labor productivity is first defined as revenue per employee. Capital productivity is also provisionally defined as revenue divided by the aggregate of *capital (tangibles)* and *capital (intangibles)*. Capital (K) is defined according to Equation (2.3.5). Then, the investment (x) is defined as the level of capital for the year less lagged capital in the previous year. The capital productivity is regressed by size class with independent variables such as capital (K) and investment (x). The labor productivity is regressed by knowledge spillover, external knowledge, and purchased technology to determine the parameter (ρ)[8] for the entire service sector. Revenue is estimated based on variables such as *software* and *KIS*.

The same procedures are applied for data on unlisted companies. In this case, detailed data on *capital (tangibles)*, *capital (intangibles)*, *R&D*, *software*, or *KIS* are unavailable. Therefore, these variables are not used in regressions. The major variables used in this analysis are *capital*, *employee*, *age*, and *exit* in logarithmic forms. The first procedure is to perform regression in stepwise method, in which dependent variable is revenue, and independent variables are *capital*, *employee*, and *age*. The second procedure is to perform the same regression by *NSC*. Olley and Pakes model and Levinsohn and Petrin model cannot be used due to the lack of data on intermediate inputs. Therefore, instrumental variables (IV) are used in place. In this case, *capital* is used as endogenous variable, *employee²* is used as IV. *Exit* and *age* are used as state variables. As an option, fixed effect is also studied with Hausman test to suffice the entire analyses on unlisted firms. The details of these dependent and independent variables are summarized in tables titled as 'Summary of regression results for listed companies' and 'Summary of regression results for unlisted companies' for each sector.

---

[8] The parameter is derived as a result of analyses performed on the following non-manufacturing sectors in Nikkei Needs database: Land transportation (5050), Sea transportation (5100), Air transportation (5150), Storage and transportation (5200), Information and Telecommunication (5250), Wholesale (6050), Retail (6100), Real estate (8050), and Service (9050). The number in parenthesis is Tokyo Stock Exchange industry code.

As for the macroeconomic analysis, the main focus is to use the parameter (ρ), which is determined from the firm-level analysis. The parameter of ρ is measured, weighted, and fed into this macroeconomic analysis over the dataset period. Another focus is to utilize the data on intermediate service inputs. The ratio of service inputs to total intermediaries is used for this purpose. The third focus is to utilize the data on ICT capital versus Non-ICT capital. The same way as the intermediate service inputs, the ratio of ICT stock to Non-ICT stock is used in the analysis. Data on ICT consumption and Non-ICT consumption are also incorporated into the analysis.

The first procedure is to regress gross output with independent variables such as capital and labor. The second procedure is to regress gross output with lagged value-added and ICT investment (x). The third procedure is to regress gross output with intermediate service inputs, capital (K) and labor (L). The fourth procedure is to regress gross output with the total of ICT consumption and Non-ICT consumption, and the total of intermediate service inputs and the other types of intermediate inputs. In the third and fourth procedures, the parameter (ρ) is reflected in the models. All procedures except for the third one is performed by multiple regressions. The third procedure is performed by IV model. Gross output estimated in the third and fourth procedures are going to be used for the final procedure of simulation. In the simulation, ICT stock, intermediate service inputs, and/or ICT consumption are adjusted upward and downward to find the impact on macro economy.

Table 4. Industry code

Industry Code (33 classes) by Tokyo Stock Exchange	Description	Category: Manufacturing (1); Non-manufacturing (2)
3650	Electronics	1 (Alternative)
5250	Information and Telecommunication	2
6050	Wholesale	2
6100	Retail	2
8050	Real estate	2
9050	Service	2

Note: In the analysis section below, result for each industry is ordered alphabetically. The three manufacturing sectors are also analyzed to make a good comparative study.

Table 5. Description of variables (1) Firm-level analysis:
Listed companies

Name	Description	Unit
Firm code	Unique firm identification number	N.A.
Year	Year when the specific data are entered	N.A.
List (flag)	1: Traded. 0: Not traded or stop being traded.	Dummy
Nikkei industry code	Classification according to Industry Code (33 classes) by Tokyo Stock Exchange	N.A.
Affiliated company	Number of affiliated company	Real
Tangible fixed assets	Total of tangible fixed assets, land, and allowance for funds used during construction	Millions of Japanese yen
Intangible fixed assets	Total of goodwill, patent, industrial new design, software, consolidated adjustment account, and other intangible fixed assets	Millions
Patent	Exclusive rights owned by firms based on Patent Law and Utility Model Act	Millions
Assets total	Total of current assets, fixed assets, and consolidated adjustment account	Millions
Operating income	Sales from merchandise, products, amount of completed work, sales income in industries such as transportation, storage, broadcasting, electricity, gas, entertainment, and sales revenue in industries such as trust, securities, and futures	Millions
Current income	Operating and nonoperating income less costs, sales expenditures, administration overhead, and nonoperating expenditures	Millions
Revenue	Net income after tax	Millions
Export and sales profits	Income from exports, amount of work completed in overseas, and operation of hotels and technical assistance and transfer	Millions
R&D	Research and development (R&D) expenditures including depreciation	Millions
Software	Amount paid for programs, system specifications, and related documentation such as flowcharts to run on computers	Millions
Capital expenditures	Capital investment	Millions
Employee	Consolidated number of employees including those working as full-time, dispatched to the firm, exclusive of trade union, leave of absence, board members with multiple appointments, temporary, and dispatched to the other firm who incur human resource costs	Person
Sales fees	Total of sales fees, promotion fees, and provision for accrued fees dealer, wholesaler, sales agents and designated sales agents	Millions
Marketing	Expenditures paid for advertisement, marketing, promotion and expansion	Millions
Patent and design	Payment for the use of patent and design	Millions
Age	Distance from 2009 (Age = 2009 − year(date))	Real
Exit	Firms not surviving for more than seven years during 1991 and 2009	Dummy

Source: Nikkei Needs Databases (Balance Sheet; Profit and Loss; Cash Flow). Data are taken in December 2009.

Table 6. Description of variables (2) Firm-level analysis:
Unlisted companies

Name	Description	Unit
Firm Code	Unique firm identification number	N.A.
Year	Year when the specific data are entered	N.A.
Industry code	Classification according to Industry Code (33 classes) by Tokyo Stock Exchange	N.A.
Capital	Capital stock paid-in.	Millions of Japanese yen
Profit	Sales from merchandise, products, amount of completed work, sales income in industries such as transportation, storage, broadcasting, electricity, gas, entertainment, and sales revenue in industries such as trust, finance, and futures	Millions
Revenue	Net income after tax	Millions
Capital expenditures	Capital investment corresponding to capital less lagged and depreciated capital stock	Millions
Employee	Number of employees not including those working as part-timer and board members on single entity basis (not consolidated)	Person
Age	Distance from 2009 (Age = 2009 – year(date))	Real
Exit	Firms not surviving for seven years during the dataset period from 2003 through 2009	Dummy

Source: Toyo Keizai Databases on unlisted companies based on quarterly journal published by Toyo Keizai Inc. The number of firms in the database ranges from 15,000 to 20,000. Data are taken in January 2010.

Table 7. Description of variables (3): Macroeconomic analysis

Name	Description	Unit
Year	Year when the specific data are entered	N.A.
Gross output	Gross output at current basic prices	Millions of Japanese yen
Intermediate inputs	Intermediate inputs at current purchasers' prices	Millions
Intermediate service inputs	Intermediate service inputs at current purchasers' prices	Millions
Value added	Gross value added at current basic prices	Millions
Employee	Number of employees	Thousands
Hours of work	Total hours worked by employee	Millions
ICT capital formation	Nominal gross fixed capital formation of ICT assets. ICT includes computing equipment, communications equipment, and software	Millions
Non ICT capital formation	Nominal gross fixed capital formation of Non-ICT assets including transport equipment, other machinery and equipment, residential structures, and other assets	Millions
ICT stock	Real fixed ICT capital stock	1995 prices
Non ICT stock	Real fixed Non-ICT capital stock	1995 prices
All stock	Real fixed capital stock of all assets	1995 prices
ICT consumption	Consumption of fixed ICT capital	1995 prices
Non-ICT consumption	Consumption of fixed Non-ICT capital	1995 prices
All consumption	Consumption of fixed capital of all assets	1995 prices
Taxes	Other taxes minus subsidies on production	Millions
Return on capital	Industry rate of return on capital	%
Depreciation rates of ICT assets	Geometric depreciation rates of ICT assets	%
Depreciation rates of other assets	Geometric depreciation rates of other assets	%
Compensation	Compensation of employees	Millions
Capital productivity	Capital productivity (mean of all service industries) obtained from the analysis on listed firms	N.A.
Labor productivity	Labor productivity (mean of all service industries) obtained from the analysis on listed firms	N.A.
Parameter for knowledge investment	Value of I/Y obtained from the analysis on listed firms	N.A.
Parameter for purchased knowledge	Value of E/Y obtained from the analysis on listed firms	N.A.
Parameter for intra-industry knowledge spillover	Value of S/Y obtained from the analysis on listed firms	N.A.
Parameter for all knowledge formulation patterns	Value estimated based on the three variables above obtained from the analysis on listed firms	N.A.

Source: EU KLEMS database, Japan, November 2009 release.

Consumption is determined based on the level of capital productivity with the efficiency (ρ) term. Labor is defined based on the same efficiency (ρ) and labor productivity. The first procedure is to regress gross output with independent variables such as capital, consumption, and the investment into IT. The second procedure is to regress gross output with independent variables such as intermediate service inputs and the investment into IT. The third procedure is to regress gross output capital, labor, and the investment into IT. Capital, consumption and gross output are detrended and used for the forth procedure, in which detrended output is regressed by consumption and IT investment. Revenue estimated in these four procedures is going to be used for the final procedure of simulation. In the simulation, ICT capital formation, service inputs, and/or ICT consumption are adjusted upward and downward to find the impact on macro economy.

As for the overall trends of Japanese economy during the dataset period from the 1990s through 2000s, please refer to the following (Yoshikawa & Miyakawa, 2009; Morikawa 2010). At the beginning of the 1990s, the high growth period of the Japanese economy, so-called 'Bubble Economy,' ended, and the economy slumped into a long-term recession. While manufacturing, agriculture and fisheries, metals, and construction sectors started to exhibit a negative growth, retail, wholesale, and service sectors were showing a positive upward trend. Japan experienced a serious financial crisis in 1997 and 1998, which worsened the growth pattern of the Japanese economy. The last half of the 1990s only showed 1.2% of growth on average. This minor growth rate was barely maintained by the growth of public sector. Service sector maintained a positive trend although retail and wholesale turned into a negative growth. In the 2000s, service, finance and insurance, and real estate remained on a positive growth path. However, the Japanese economy suffered from deflationary pressures, which had the economy turn into the first negative growth in the post-war period. Due to the collapse of the Bubble Economy and the financial crisis in the 1990s, financial sector and real estate in Japan were not able to achieve a strong turnaround. Therefore, the other service sectors than financial sectors became leading sectors as a driving force for the whole Japanese economy. As for the labor market, one distinguishing trend in Japan since the 1990s had been the increase of part-time workers. According to labor statistics, part-time workers increased from approximately 5 million in 1990 to 8.2 million in 2008. Wage for workers on average, therefore, had been lowered over the dataset period.

3.2. RESULT OF MICROECONOMIC ANALYSIS

Please refer to the following instructions first for how to read figures showing the results of each industry analysis.

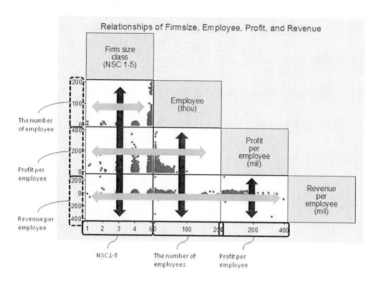

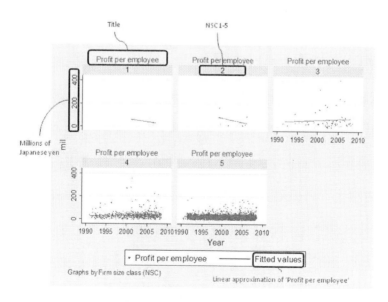

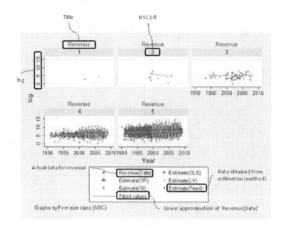

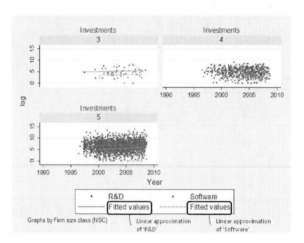

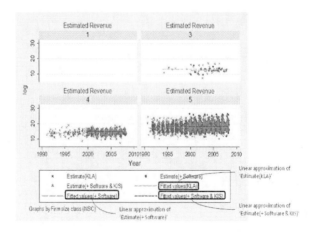

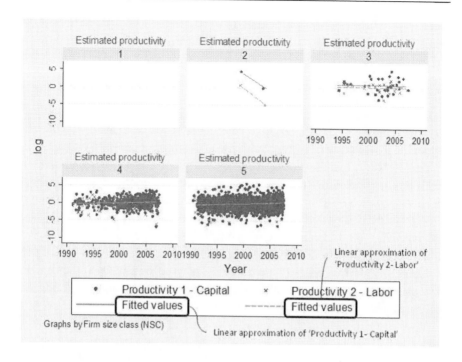

Graphs by Firm size class (NSC)

3.2.1. Industry: Electronics

Analysis (1)
Type of firm: Listed
Time series: 1991-2008 (year)
Number of firms: 347
Number of observations:

NSC	Freq.	Percent	Cum.
1	2	0.05	0.05
2	8	0.21	0.26
3	57	1.51	1.77
4	643	17.02	18.79
5	3,068	81.21	100
Total	3,778	100	

Observation
   According to Table 8, *capital (tangibles)* and *R&D* give the largest impacts on the change in R2. According to Table 9, *age* and age^2 are

significant with negative coefficients in all cases (Model 1, 2, 5, 6, 8, 9, 10, and 13). Olley and Pakes method presents that firms in this sector focuses on *R&D* as input and *patent* as output (Model 7) while *KIS* and *capital (tangibles)* become also important when firms engage in trade (Model 8). Levinsohn and Petrin method also shows that *KIS* is statistically significant with firms engaging in trade (Model 10). When firms engage in R&D, *capital (tangibles)*, *employee*, and *age* (with negative coefficients) are statistically significant (Model 6). This trend is typically seen in previous literatures that have investigated into manufacturing sectors in terms of business size, innovation, and output. According to Figure 9 and onward, profit per employee is increasing with NSC 3 and 4. Revenue shows growth with NSC 3 through 5 during the dataset period. Revenue with trade is growing most with NSC 3, and revenue with trade and revenue with R&D are also growing with NSC 4 and 5. Investments into R&D and software have been highest with NSC 5. The gap between the two types of investment seems to be consistent across firm size classes, and the level of investments is growing for both R&D and software. The impact of *software* and *KIS* together turns from negative to positive as firm size class goes across from 3 to 4. However, the impact of *software* only stays on the leveled ground or turns into negative. In line with these trends, *capital (intangibles)* are statistically significant with negative coefficients (Model 4 and 5). Labor productivity is growing more strongly compared to capital productivity. It is suggestive that firms grow most with NSC 3 to 4, and that once *software* and *KIS* reach a certain level, *software* and *KIS* start giving a positive impact on revenue for firms in NSC 5. It is supposed that this sector maintains revenue growth as business size expands while the factors for the growth can be supported partly by *KIS*. It means that large firms have heterogeneous factors to grow and engage in trade and R&D, and that they invest into R&D to maintain competitiveness with the support of increasing investment into *software*.

Table 8. Impact on R-squared for listed companies: Electronics

	(1)	(2)	(3)	(4)
Additional variables	Capital (tangibles)	Capital (intangibles)	R&D	Age
Observations	484	483	357	379
R-squared	0.695	0.675	0.722	0.675
Change in R-squared	0.0539	0.0293	0.0418	0.0133

Note: Dependent variable: Revenue.. Independent variable (default): Employee.

Electronics

Table 9. Summary of regression results for listed companies: Electronics

Model / REGRESSION	(1) OLS	(2) OLS: Trade	(3) OLS: R&D	(4) OLS: NSC 4	(5) OLS: NSC 5	(6) OLS: Size	(7) OP	(8) OP: Trade	(9) LP	(10) LP: Trade	(11) IV	(12) IV: Trade	(13) Fixed Effect
Independent Variables	Capital (tangibles), Capital (intangibles), Employee, Age	For firms engaging in Trade: Capital (tangibles), Capital (intangibles), Employee, Age, Trade	For firms engaging in R&D Capital (tangibles), Capital (intangibles), Employee, Age, Patent	Capital (tangibles), Capital (intangibles), Employee, Age, Patent	Capital (tangibles), Capital (intangibles), Employee, Age, Patent	For firms engaging in R&D Capital (intangibles), Employee, Age, $Employee^2$, Age^2, Patent, NSC categorical dummies (1-5)	Est, Age, Employee, KIS, R&D, Patent, Capital (tangibles), Capital (intangibles)	For firms engaging in Trade: Est, Age, Employee, KIS, R&D, Patent, Capital (tangibles), Capital (intangibles)	State variables (Employee, Age), Proxy variable (KIS), Capital (KIS); Capital (Tangibles, Intangibles)	For firms engaging in Trade: Employee, Age, KIS, Capital (tangibles), Capital (intangibles)	Instrumental variables (Software, KIS), Endogenous (Capital (tangibles), Capital (intangibles), Employee)	For firms engaging in Trade: Instrumental variables (Software, KIS), Endogenous (Capital (tangibles), Capital (intangibles), Employee)	For firms engaging in R&D: Capital (tangibles), Capital (intangibles), Employee, $Employee^2$, Age^2
Capital (tangibles)	0.441*** (0.0467)	0.445*** (0.0569)			0.829*** (0.163)	0.462*** (0.0387)	-0.283 (0.286)	0.344*** (0.130)					0.0735 (0.115)
Capital (intangibles)	0.0417** (0.0203)			-0.654** (0.266)	-0.233* (0.138)	0.0354* (0.0192)	-0.414 (0.359)	-0.203** (0.0806)					0.0447 (0.0278)
R&D							0.380*** (0.127)	0.159*** (0.0513)					0.115*** (0.0400)
Employee	0.298*** (0.0448)	0.149** (0.0631)	0.573*** (0.118)				0.460 (0.356)	0.0718 (0.153)	-0.0270 (0.164)	-0.0375 (0.159)			
Age	-0.569*** (0.106)	-0.595*** (0.142)			-0.798* (0.431)		0.418 (0.858)	-0.667** (0.263)	-0.744*** (0.165)	-0.648*** (0.209)			
Trade		0.224*** (0.0512)											
$Employee^2$						0.167*** (0.0207)		0.152* (0.0805)					0.137** (0.0582)
Age^2						-0.285*** (0.0521)							-0.239*** (0.0356)
NSC 3						0.0629 (0.680)							
NSC 4						-0.875 (0.644)							
NSC 5						-1.017 (0.650)							
Est							0.604 (0.581)	-0.124 (0.313)					
Software							0.110 (0.153)				-0.538*** (0.133)	-0.969*** (0.296)	
Patent							0.259** (0.108)						
KIS							0.178 (0.127)	0.147** (0.0570)	0.136 (0.416)	0.636* (0.386)	1.388*** (0.187)	2.045*** (0.470)	
Capital (total)									1*** (0.371)	0.437 (0.399)			
Constant	0.802*** (0.225)	-0.283 (0.341)	2.709*** (0.939)	9.151*** (1.375)	1.088 (1.140)	1.349** (0.666)	3.888*** (1.483)	1.637** (0.754)			1.589*** (0.533)	0.715 (1.226)	3.599*** (1.035)
Observations	1917	756	66	9	57	1917	27	149	300	166	352	209	1626
R-squared	0.471	0.496	0.324	0.450	0.439	0.477	0.367	0.426			-0.279	-1.691	0.097
Number of firms													276

Note: Robust standard errors in parentheses. *** p<0.01, ** p<0.05, * p<0.1

Legend: Ordinary Least Square (OLS), Olley and Pakes method (OP), Levinsohn and Petrin method (LP), Instrumental variable (IV).

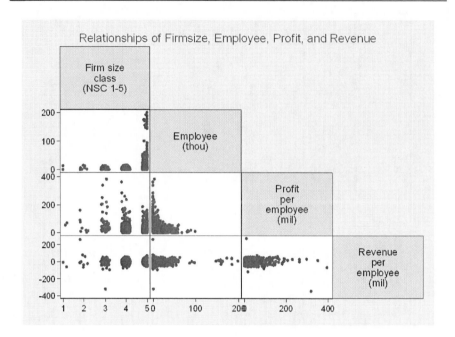

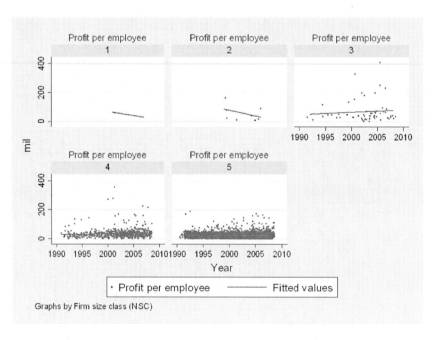

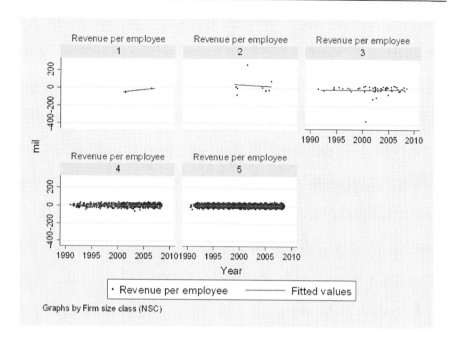

Graphs by Firm size class (NSC)

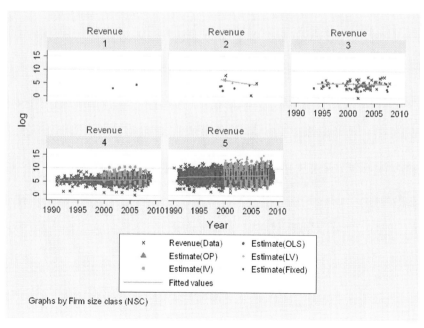

Graphs by Firm size class (NSC)

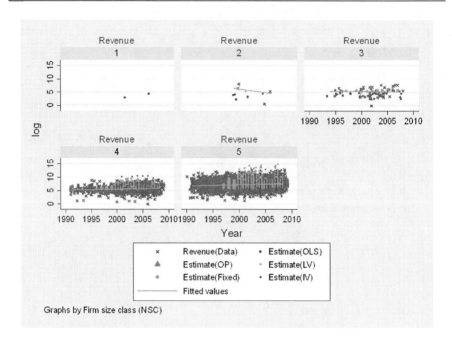

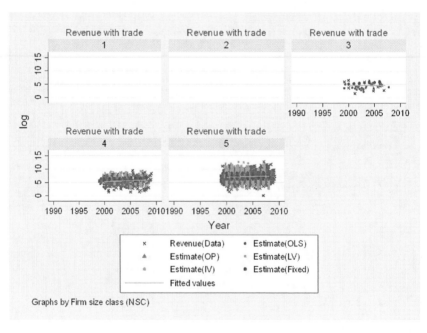

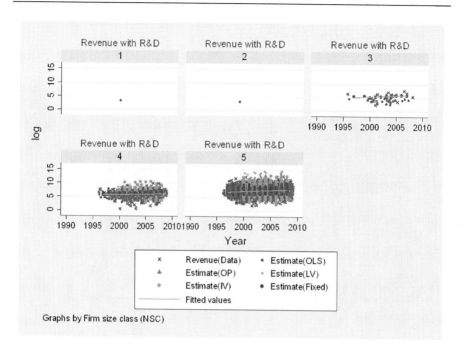

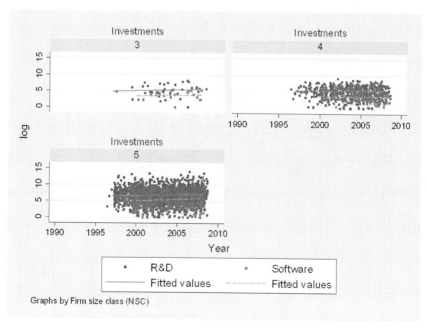

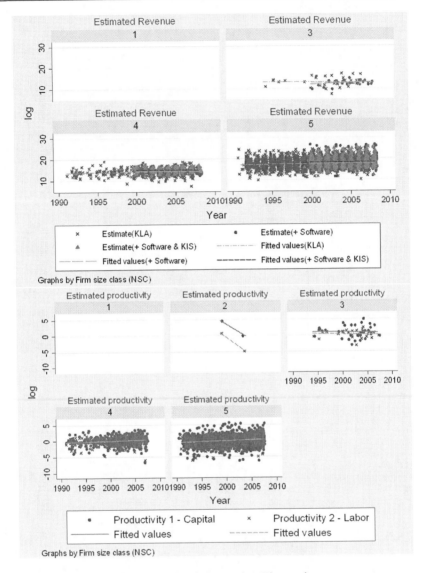

Figure 9. Summary of analysis for listed companies: Electronics.

Analysis (2)
    Type of firm: Unlisted
    Time series: 2003-2009 (year)
    Number of firms: 353
    Number of observations: 1,323

Observation

According to Table 10, the coefficient for *capital* is lowest and the coefficient for *employee* is highest with NSC 4 (Model 4). According to Figure 10, there is a similar trend in terms of revenue growth, which starts growing with NSC 3. Interestingly enough, the trend of revenue growth follows the same pattern as the trend of productivity growth. It is supposed that the impact of *capital* becomes smallest with NSC 4, and labor productivity is growing as firm sizes become larger, whose impact is largest with NSC 4. Profit per employee, revenue per employee and productivity dispersions are largest with NSC 4. It is supposed that firms in NSC 4 need to be observed closely to clarify the growth pattern of unlisted firms in the electronics sector.

Table 20. Summary of regression results for unlisted companies: Electronics

Electronics

Model	(1)	(2)	(3)	(4)	(5)	(6)	(7)
REGRESSION	OLS	OLS: NSC 1	OLS: NSC 3	OLS: NSC 4	OLS: NSC 5	OLS: Size	Fixed effect
Independent Variables	Capital, Age, Employee	Capital, Employee	Capital, Employee	Capital, Employee	Capital, Employee	Capital, Employee, Employee^2, Age^2, NSC categorical dummies (1-5)	Capital, Age, Employee, Employee^2, Age^2
Capital	0.241***	0.633***	0.365***	0.105*	0.332***	0.243***	0.0108
	(0.0368)	(0.145)	(0.116)	(0.0585)	(0.0612)	(0.0375)	(0.206)
Employee^2						0.459***	0.0792
						(0.0458)	(0.102)
Age^2						-0.295***	-0.321***
						(0.0566)	(0.0448)
NSC 2						-0.292	
						(0.358)	
NSC 3						-0.318	
						(0.303)	
NSC 4						-0.358	
						(0.376)	
NSC 5						-0.622	
						(0.483)	
Age	-0.592***						
	(0.124)						
Employee	0.833***		0.794***	0.920***	0.816***		
	(0.0431)		(0.279)	(0.147)	(0.144)		
Constant	0.0501	-0.303	-1.277	-0.547	-1.456*	-0.0113	5.025***
	(0.252)	(0.478)	(1.097)	(0.792)	(0.767)	(0.332)	(1.493)
Observations	1023	33	185	492	286	1023	1023
R-squared	0.559	0.379	0.110	0.091	0.426	0.561	0.069
Number of firmid							306

Note: Robust standard errors in parentheses. *** p<0.01, ** p<0.05, * p<0.1
Legend: Ordinary Least Square (OLS).

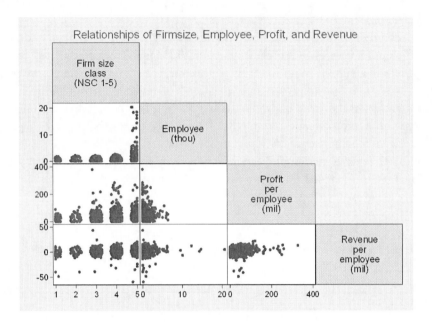

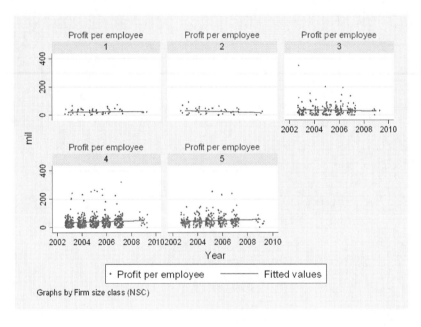

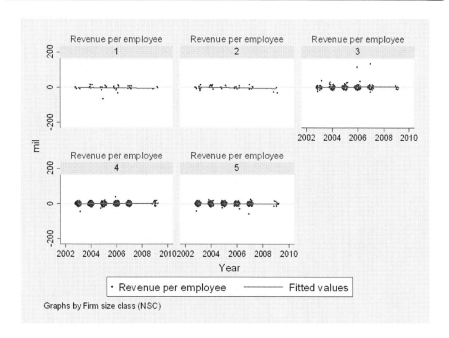

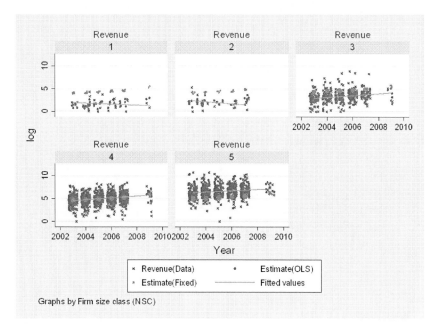

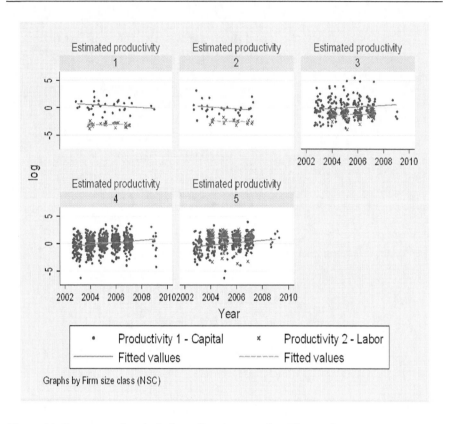

Figure 10. Summary of analysis for unlisted companies: Electronics.

3.2.2. Industry: Information and Telecommunication

Analysis (1)
Type of firm: Listed
Time series: 1991-2008 (year)
Number of firms: 338
Number of observations:

NSC	Freq.	Percent	Cum.
1	3	0.23	0.23
2	9	0.7	0.94
3	192	15.01	15.95
4	467	36.51	52.46
5	608	47.54	100
Total	1,279	100	

Observation

Capital (tangibles) and *R&D* have importance in the determination of R2 according to Table 11. For firms engaging in trade, *exit* is statistically significant in Olley and Pakes model (Model 8). According to Figure 11, revenue starts growing with NSC 3 although large firms have not been able to maintain growth unless they engage in trade. The investment into software is, obviously, larger than R&D. However, the level of expenditures for both software and R&D seem lowering in recent years particularly with NSC 5. Firms performing R&D shows a negative revenue trend with NSC 5, whose trend curve is similar to the investment curve as well as estimated revenue curve. The impact of *KIS* shows a strong positive trend even with NSC 5. Labor productivity shows a negative growth in NSC 5. Therefore, the use and purchase of external knowledge seems to be helpful for supporting productivity according to the regression results (Model 9, 11, and 12).

**Table 31. Impact on R-squared for listed companies:
Information and Telecommunication**

	(1)	(2)	(3)	(4)
Additional variables	Capital (tangibles)	Capital (intangibles)	R&D	Age
Observations	976	976	415	613
R-squared	0.590	0.554	0.581	0.518
Change in R-squared	0.0774	0.0408	0.061	0.0002

Note: Dependent variable: Revenue.. Independent variable (default): Employee.

Table 42. Summary of regression results for listed companies: Information and Telecommunication

Information and Telecommunication

Model	(1)	(2)	(3)	(4)	(5)	(6)	(7)	(8)	(9)	(10)	(11)	(12)	(13)
REGRESSION	OLS	OLS: Trade	OLS: R&D	OLS: NSC 3	OLS: NSC 4	OLS: NSC 5	OP	OP: Trade	LP	LP: Trade	IV	IV: Trade	Fixed Effect
Independent Variables	Capital (tangibles), Capital (intangibles), Employee, Age	For firms engaging in Trade: Capital (tangibles), Capital (intangibles), Employee, Age, Trade	For firms engaging in R&D: Capital (tangibles), Capital (intangibles), Employee, Age, Patent	Capital (tangibles), Capital (intangibles), Employee, Age, Patent	Capital (tangibles), Capital (intangibles), Employee, Age, Patent	Capital (tangibles), Capital (intangibles), Employee, Age, Patent	Ext, Age, Employee, KIS, R&D, Patent, Capital (tangibles), Capital (intangibles)	For firms engaging in Trade: Ext, Age, Employee, KIS, R&D, Patent, Capital (tangibles), Capital (intangibles)	State variables (Employee, Age), Proxy variable (KIS), Capital (Tangibles, Intangibles)	For firms engaging in Trade: Employee, Age, KIS, Capital (tangibles), Capital (intangibles)	Instrumental variables (Software, KIS), Endogenous (Capital (tangibles), Capital (intangibles), Employee)	For firms engaging in Trade: Instrumental variables (Software, KIS), Endogenous (Capital (tangibles), Capital (intangibles), Employee)	For firms engaging in R&D: Capital (tangibles), Capital (intangibles), Employee^2, Age^2
Capital (tangibles)	0.253*** (0.0264)	0.235*** (0.0411)	0.243*** (0.0278)	0.240*** (0.0571)	0.242*** (0.0522)	0.227*** (0.0535)		-0.0426 (0.137)					0.207* (0.125)
Capital (intangibles)	0.154*** (0.0290)	0.0881** (0.0358)	0.121*** (0.0296)	0.170*** (0.0566)	0.170***	0.142*** (0.0376)		0.257** (0.112)					0.0103 (0.0652)
Employee^2			0.303*** (0.0369)										0.0257 (0.121)
Age^2			-0.166* (0.0971)										-0.114* (0.0692)
NSC 2			0.045 (1.147)										
NSC 3			-1.01 (0.833)										
NSC 4			-1.727** (0.846)										
NSC 5			-2.148** (0.88)										
Employee	0.348*** (0.0454)	0.436*** (0.0658)		0.818** (0.367)	0.621*** (0.204)	0.571*** (0.0778)		0.388 (0.363)	0.302** (0.140)	0.557 (0.341)	0.0696 (0.0609)	-0.292 (0.270)	
Software							-0.0409 (0)						
Patent							-1.522 (0)						
Ext								0.864* (0.419)					
Age								0.283 (0.750)	-0.257 (0.543)	-0.299 (0.809)			
R&D								-0.0427 (0.229)					-0.0507 (0.0671)
KIS								-0.216 (0.165)	1*** (0.343)	0 (0.397)	0.490*** (0.0884)	1.099*** (0.353)	
Trade								0.493* (0.268)					
Capital (total)									0.598 (0.390)	1** (0.432)			
Constant	1.514*** (0.198)	1.353*** (0.277)	2.134*** (0.818)	0.677 (1.464)	-0.0687 (1.164)	0.0982 (0.401)	8.367 (0)	-1.573 (1.001)			3.127*** (0.357)	3.102*** (0.499)	5.136*** (1.307)
Observations	613	363	613	81	194	334	3	30	105	46	127	55	415
R-squared	0.613	0.558	0.63	0.263	0.213	0.657	1.000	0.798			0.473	0.069	0.050
Number of firms													156

Note: Robust standard errors in parentheses. *** $p<0.01$, ** $p<0.05$, * $p<0.1$

Legend: Ordinary Least Square (OLS), Olley and Pakes method (OP), Levinsohn and Petrin method (LP), Instrumental variable (IV).

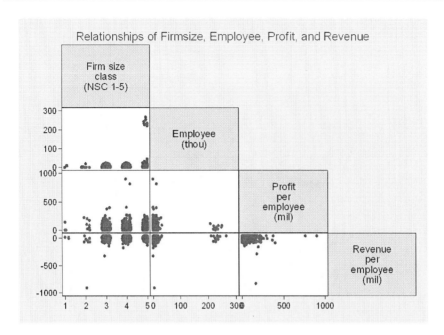

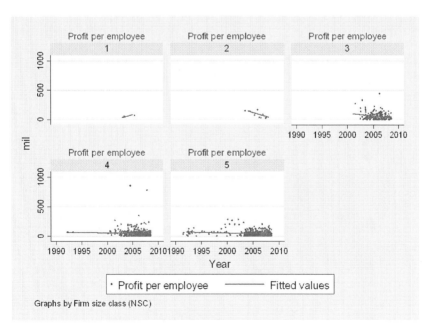

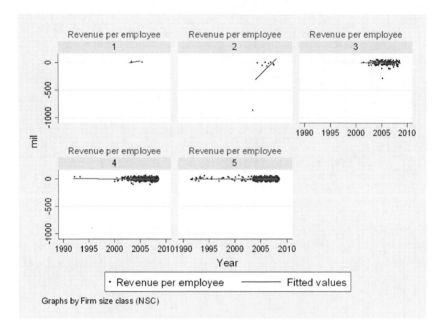

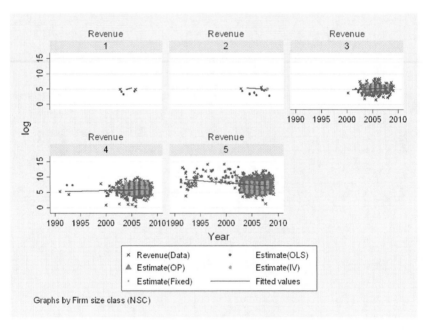

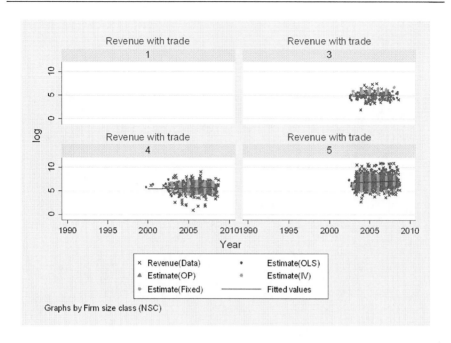

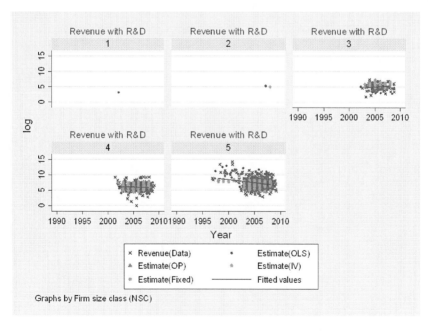

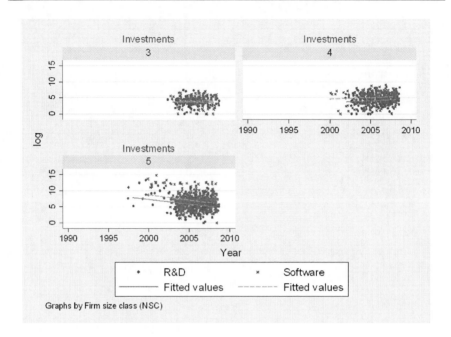

Graphs by Firm size class (NSC)

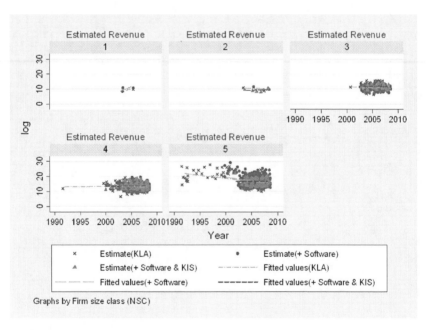

Graphs by Firm size class (NSC)

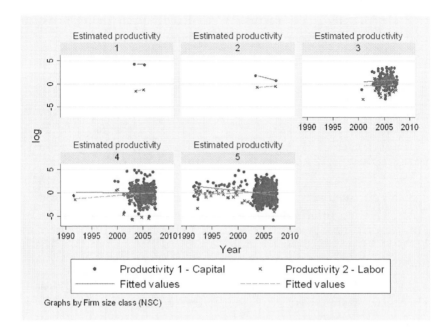

Figure 11. Summary of analysis for listed companies: Information and Telecommunication.

Analysis (2)
Type of firm: Unlisted
Time series: 2003-2009 (year)
Number of firms: 579
Number of observations: 722.

Observation

According to Table 13, the coefficients for *capital* and *labor* are lower for NSC 4 compared to NSC 3 and 5 according to OLS regressions (Model 1-4). According to Figure 12, profit per employee is obviously declining with all firm size classes. The distribution of both profit per employee and revenue per employee is becoming smaller in recent years, however, the gap of revenue by itself among firms are becoming larger in recent years. Revenue shows growth for NSC 1 and 2, and decline for NSC 3, 4, and 5. Capital productivity shows a downward trend, however, the level of labor productivity is gradually improved as firm size becomes large. Therefore, the effective utilization of labor and intermediaries may be important, which may support stable labor productivity growth.

Table 53. Summary of regression results for unlisted companies: Information and Telecommunication

	(1)	(2)	(3)	(4)
Additional variables	Capital (tangibles)	Capital (intangibles)	R&D	Age
Observations	976	976	415	613
R-squared	0.590	0.554	0.581	0.518
Change in R-squared	0.0774	0.0408	0.061	0.0002

Note: Dependent variable: Revenue.. Independent variable (default): Employee.

Table 64. Summary of regression results for unlisted companies: Information and Telecommunication

Information & Telecommunication

Model	(1)	(2)	(3)	(4)	(5)	(6)
REGRESSION	OLS	OLS: NSC 3	OLS: NSC 4	OLS: NSC 5	OLS: Size	Fixed effect
Independent Variables	Capital, Age, Employee	Capital, Employee	Capital, Employee	Capital, Employee	Capital, Employee, Employee^2, Age^2, NSC categorical dummies (1-5)	Capital, Age, Employee, Employee^2, Age^2
Capital	0.535*** (0.0406)	0.631*** (0.0841)	0.484*** (0.0576)	0.517*** (0.0553)	0.519*** (0.0366)	0.0230 (0.275)
Employee^2					0.415*** (0.0592)	0.204* (0.111)
Age^2					0.174** (0.0690)	0.0211 (0.0498)
NSC 2					-1.238* (0.650)	
NSC 3					-1.727*** (0.630)	
NSC 4					-1.357* (0.708)	
NSC 5					-1.553* (0.828)	
Age	0.360*** (0.128)					
Employee	0.812*** (0.0456)	0.856*** (0.259)	0.680*** (0.224)	0.835*** (0.166)		
Constant	-2.569*** (0.299)	-3.010*** (0.965)	-1.027 (1.166)	-2.255** (1.071)	-1.040* (0.631)	2.727 (1.701)
Observations	563	174	189	171	563	563
R-squared	0.673	0.349	0.351	0.513	0.682	0.041
Number of firmid						474

Note: Robust standard errors in parentheses. *** p<0.01, ** p<0.05, * p<0.1

Legend: Ordinary Least Square (OLS).

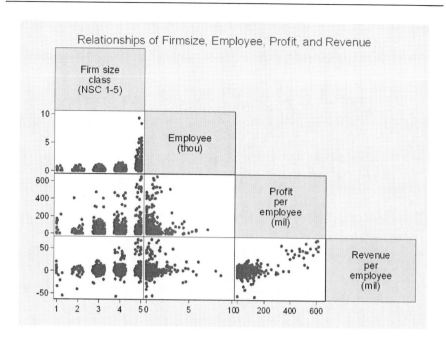

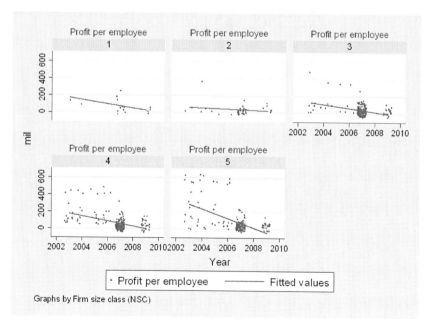

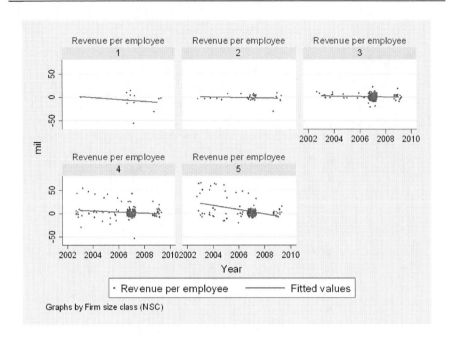

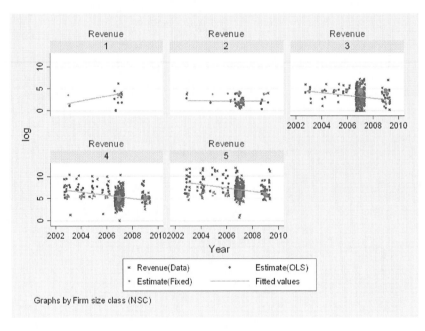

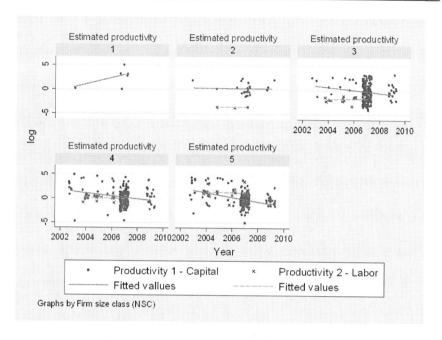

Figure 12. Summary of analysis for unlisted companies: Information and Telecommunication.

3.2.3. Industry: Real estate

Analysis (1)
Type of firm: Listed
Time series: 1991-2008 (year)
Number of firms: 143
Number of observations:

NSC	Freq.	Percent	Cum.
2	3	0.31	0.31
3	138	14.27	14.58
4	487	50.36	64.94
5	339	35.06	100
Total	967	100	

Observation

According to Table 15, *age* gives the largest impacts on the change in R2 with negative coefficient while *capital (intangibles)* comes next. According to Table 16, *employee* is related to revenue growth also when firms are engaging in trade (Model 1 and 2). According to Figure 13, revenue per employee grows when firms are in NSC 3. The dispersion of revenue per employee is very small, which means that the gap of revenue among firms is small. However, the revenue by itself is showing a dispersed trend especially in NSC 4 in recent years. *Trade* and *R&D* seem effective in terms of raising revenues when firm size is NSC 3 and/or 4 but not NSC 5. In these size classes of NSC 3 and 4, R&D expenditures and software investment are growing, in particular, with NSC 4. R&D expenditures drop when it comes to NSC 5 while software investment stays on. The impact of *KIS* is negative particularly from NSC 4 to 5. This indicates that firms in NSC 4 seek external services in addition to internal knowledge production although revenue in this size classes are not growing. The impact of *software* stays positive in NSC 3 and 4, which turns into negative in NSC 5. The positive impacts of using *KIS* and *software* seem largest with NSC 3 so as the growth of revenue per employee. It is noted that the presence of positive and negative impacts of *software* and *KIS* on revenue may be a cause for regression not to show statistical significance for either *KIS* or *software* (Model 6-11).

Table 75. Impact on R-squared for listed companies: Real Estate

	(1)	(2)	(3)	(4)
Additional variables	Capital (tangibles)	Capital (intangibles)	R&D	Age
Observations	810	809	48	520
R-squared	0.249	0.259	0.677	0.288
Change in R-squared	0.0162	0.0266	0.0132	0.0834

Note: Dependent variable: Revenue.. Independent variable (default): Employee.

Table 86. Summary of regression results for listed companies: Real Estate

Real estate

Model	(1)	(2)	(3)	(4)	(5)	(6)	(7)	(8)	(9)	(10)	(11)
REGRESSION	OLS	OLS: Trade	OLS: R&D	OLS: NSC 4	OLS: Size	OP	OP: Trade	LP	IV	IV: Trade	Fixed Effect
Independent Variables	Capital (tangibles), Capital (intangibles), Employee, Age	For firms engaging in Trade: Capital (tangibles), Capital (intangibles), Employee, Age, Trade	For firms engaging in R&D Capital (tangibles), Capital (intangibles), Employee, Age, Patent	Capital (tangibles), Capital (intangibles), Employee, Age, Patent	For firms engaging in R&D: Capital (intangibles), Age, Employee, Age^2, Employee^2, Age^2, Patent, NSC categorical dummies (1-5)	Exit, Age, Employee, KIS, Capital (tangibles), Capital (intangibles)	For firms engaging in Trade: Exit, Age, Employee, KIS, Capital (tangibles), Capital (intangibles)	State variables (Employee, Age), Proxy variable (KIS, Capital (Tangibles, Intangibles)	Instrumental variables (Software, KIS), Endogenous (Capital (tangibles), Capital (intangibles), Employee)	For firms engaging in Trade Instrumental variables (Software, KIS), Endogenous (Capital (tangibles), Capital (intangibles), Employee)	For firms engaging in R&D: Capital (tangibles), Capital (intangibles), Employee, Employee^2, Age^2
Capital (tangibles)	0.160***	0.275***		-0.708	0.163***	0.277*	-1.886				-0.663
	(0.0326)	(0.0911)		(0)	(0.0333)	(0.146)	(0)				(0.504)
Capital (intangibles)	0.0540*			0.290	0.0544*	-0.0585	3.240				1.360***
	(0.0302)			(0)	(0.0299)	(0.172)	(0)				(0.400)
R&D											0.832***
											(0.268)
Age	-1.647***	-1.026***	-5.879***	-5.162		-0.684		-0.531			
	(0.167)	(0.372)	(1.092)	(0)		(0.738)		(0.377)			
Patent			-0.661**	-1.671							
			(0.160)	(0)							
Employee	0.305***	0.384**	-1.591*	-3.767		-0.170		-0.106			
	(0.0533)	(0.150)	(0.677)	(0)		(0.293)		(0.213)			
Trade	0.143*						0.964				
	(0.0725)						(0)				
Employee^2					0.202***						-0.0604
					(0.0413)						(0.469)
Age^2					-0.828***						-0.117
					(0.0884)						(0.315)
NSC 3					0.389						
					(0.300)						
NSC 4					0.324*						
					(0.189)						
Exit						-0.124					
						(1.571)					
Software						0.0997	0.178		-0.318	-0.275	
						(0.174)	(0)		(0.358)	(0.666)	
KIS						0.211		0	1.521	-4.066	
						(0.146)		(0.396)	(0.933)	(2.696)	
Capital (total)								0.221			
								(0.414)			
Constant	4.523***	1.541***	20.21**	38.10	3.690***	4.456**	1.845		-2.132	26.88*	2.558
	(0.281)	(0.519)	(4.529)	(0)	(0.593)	(1.840)	(0)		(5.316)	(15.24)	(7.878)
Observations	520	86	8	6	520	55	5	79	80	6	48
R-squared	0.341	0.714	0.943	1.000	0.344	0.202	1.000		-1.190	0.240	0.401
Number of firmid											10

Note: Robust standard errors in parentheses *** p<0.01, ** p<0.05, * p<0.1

Legend: Ordinary Least Square (OLS) Olley and Pakes method (OP) Instrumental variable (IV).

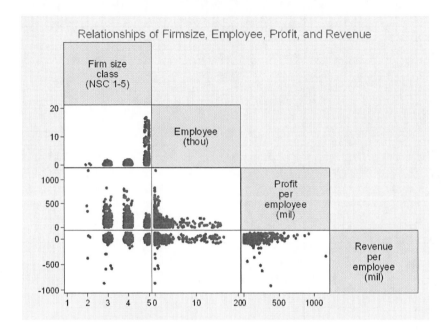

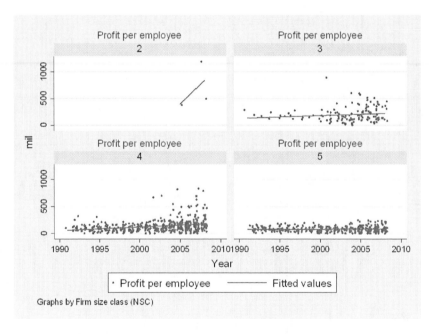

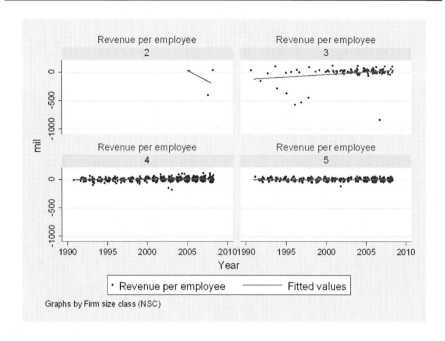

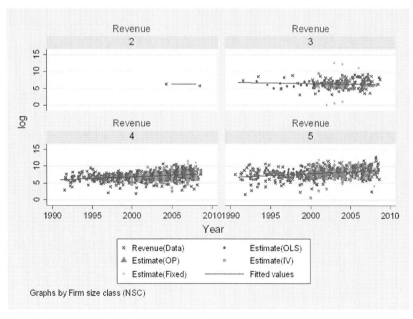

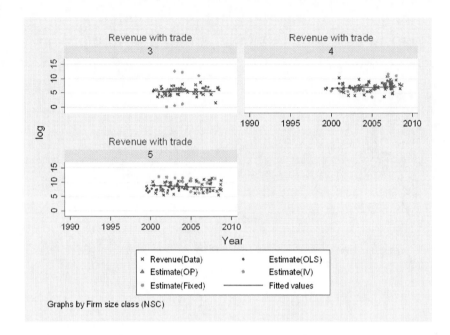

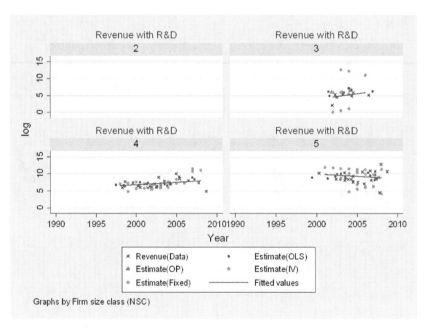

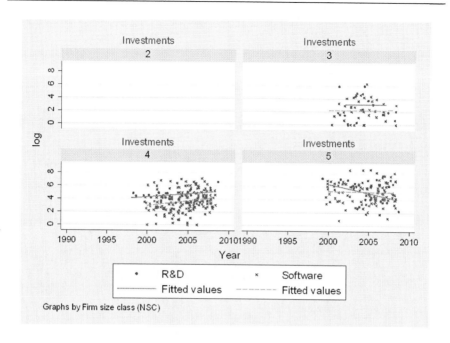

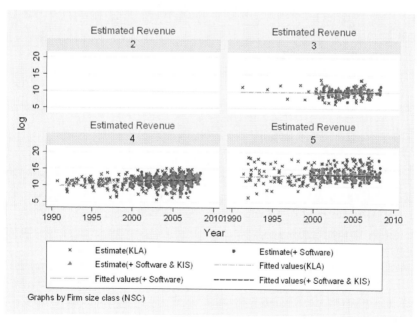

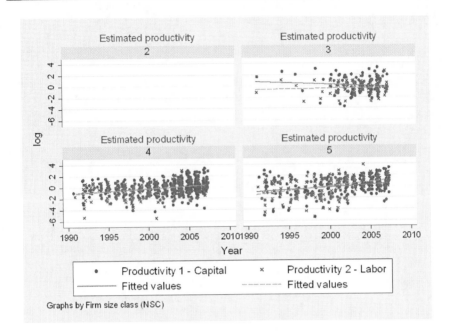

Figure 13. Summary of analysis for listed companies: Real Estate.

Analysis (2)
Type of firm: Unlisted
Time series: 2003-2009 (year)
Number of firms: 150
Number of observations: 532

Observation

According to the following table, *capital* is statistically significant in all models (Model 1-7). Besides, *age* is significant with positive coefficients for NSC 3 (Model 1 and 3). Contrary to listed firms, OLS shows that firm sizes are related to revenue trend when firms are in NSC 2 or NSC 3 (Model 6). According to the figures, however, both profit per employee and revenue per employee are on the leveled ground or showing negative trends from NSC 2 to 4. Profit per employee and revenue per employee exhibits a wide gap among firms particularly with NSC 3 and 4. The gap between labor productivity and capital productivity is largest with NSC 4. Capital productivity is related to revenue, in which NSC 4 shows the highest impact.

Table 17. Summary of regression results for unlisted companies: Real Estate

Real estate

Model	(1)	(2)	(3)	(4)	(5)	(6)	(7)
REGRESSION	OLS	OLS: NSC 1	OLS: NSC 3	OLS: NSC 4	OLS: NSC 5	OLS: Size	Fixed effect
Independent Variables	Capital, Age, Employee	Capital, Employee	Capital, Employee	Capital, Employee	Capital, Employee	Capital, Employee, Employee^2, Age^2, NSC categorical dummies (1-5)	Capital, Age, Employee, Employee^2, Age^2
Capital	0.354*** (0.0383)	2.052** (0.865)	0.340*** (0.0651)	0.418*** (0.0563)	0.306*** (0.0946)	0.349*** (0.0435)	0.194* (0.107)
Employee^2						0.305*** (0.0753)	0.287*** (0.102)
Age^2						-0.0485 (0.0749)	-0.246*** (0.0487)
NSC 2						-1.049* (0.590)	
NSC 3						-1.118* (0.581)	
NSC 4						-1.075 (0.706)	
NSC 5						-1.399 (0.900)	
Age	0.514*** (0.0685)		1.386*** (0.277)				
Constant	1.540*** (0.414)	-5.733 (4.687)	-1.948* (1.151)	3.920*** (0.378)	5.279*** (0.668)	2.359*** (0.591)	2.978*** (1.127)
Observations	478	9	198	197	56	478	478
R-squared	0.311	0.445	0.225	0.220	0.163	0.319	0.118
Number of firmid							141

Note: Robust standard errors in parentheses. *** p<0.01, ** p<0.05, * p<0.1
Legend: Ordinary Least Square (OLS).

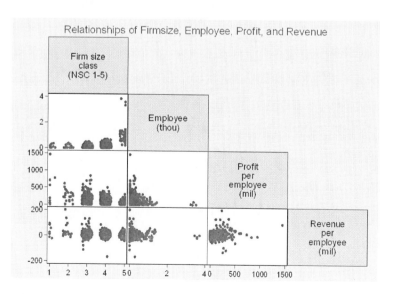

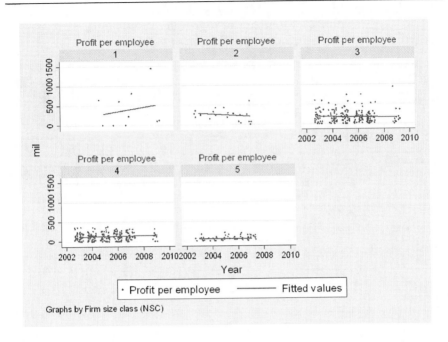

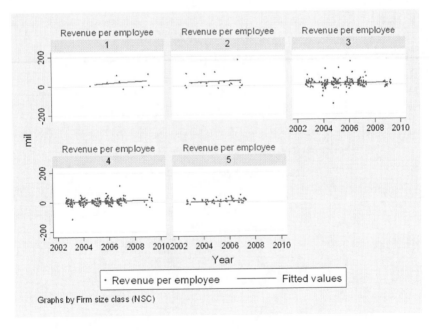

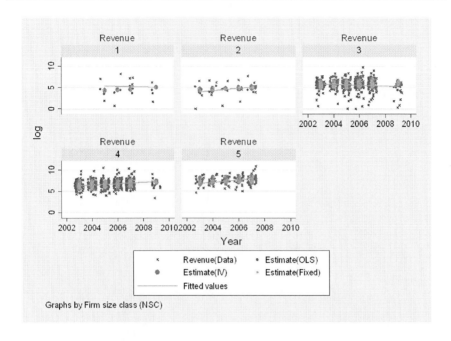

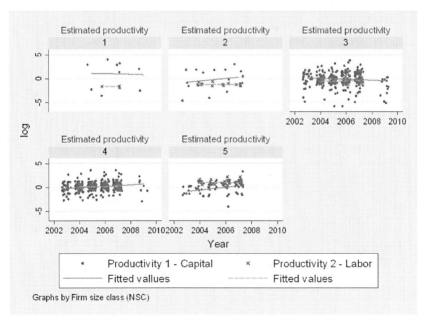

Figure 14. Summary of analysis for unlisted companies: Real Estate.

3.2.4. Industry: Retail

Analysis (1)
Type of firm: Listed
Time series: 1991-2008 (year)
Number of firms: 384
Number of observations:

NSC	Freq.	Percent	Cum.
2	1	0.03	0.03
3	32	1.1	1.13
4	710	24.33	25.46
5	2,175	74.54	100
Total	2,918	100	

Observation

According to Figure 15, *capital (intangibles)* are the most important determinant in terms or R2. According to Table 18, *capital (tangibles), capital (intangibles),* and *employee* are statistically most frequently significant in OLS models (Model 1-6). *KIS* are found significant in Olley and Pakes model whether or not firms engage in trade (Model 7 and 8). According to Figure 15, revenue with trade and R&D do not grow. R&D expenditures grow with NSC 4, and software investment continues to grow with NSC 5. It seems that the investment starts yielding turnover with NSC 5. The impact of *KIS* and *software* investment turns into positive with NSC 5, which is also shown in regressions (Model 7, 8, 11, and 12).

Table 18. Impact on R-squared for listed companies: Retail

	(1)	(2)	(3)	(4)
Additional variables	Capital (tangibles)	Capital (intangibles)	R&D	Age
Observations	2297	2297	175	1571
R-squared	0.379	0.391	0.451	0.345
Change in R-squared	0.0158	0.0278	0.011	0.0135

Note: Dependent variable: Revenue.. Independent variable (default): Employee.

Table 19. Summary of regression results for listed companies: Retail

Retail

Model / REGRESSION	(1) OLS	(2) OLS: Trade	(4) OLS: NSC 4	(5) OLS: NSC 5	(6) OLS: Size	(7) OP	(8) OP: Trade	(9) LP	(10) LP: Trade	(11) IV	(12) IV: Trade	(13) Fixed Effect
Independent Variables	Capital (tangibles), Capital (intangibles), Employee, Age	For firms engaging in Trade: Capital (tangibles), Capital (intangibles), Employee, Age, Trade	Capital (tangibles), Capital (intangibles), Employee, Age, Patent	Capital (tangibles), Capital (intangibles), Employee, Age, Patent	For firms engaging in R&D: Capital (intangibles), Capital (tangibles), Employee, Age, Employee², Patent, Age², NSC categorical dummies (1-5)	Exit, Age, Employee, KIS, Capital (tangibles), Capital (intangibles)	For firms engaging in Trade: Exit, Age, Employee, KIS, Capital (tangibles), Capital (intangibles)	State variables (Employee, Age), Proxy variable (KIS), Capital (Tangibles, Intangibles)	For firms engaging in Trade: Employee, Age, KIS, Capital (tangibles), Capital (intangibles)	Instrumental variables (Software, KIS), Endogenous (Capital (tangibles), Capital (intangibles), Employee)	For firms engaging in Trade: Instrumental variables (Software, KIS), Endogenous (Capital (tangibles), Capital (intangibles), Employee)	For firms engaging in R&D: Capital (tangibles), Capital (intangibles), Employee², Age²
Capital (tangibles)	0.218*** (0.0399)	0.493*** (0.0918)		0.318*** (0.0491)	0.236*** (0.0398)	0.0196 (0.113)	1.176 (0.746)					-0.247 (0.380)
Capital (intangibles)	0.118*** (0.0244)			0.134*** (0.0298)	0.112*** (0.0239)	0.121 (0.0964)	-0.446 (0.630)					0.276 (0.167)
Employee	0.463*** (0.0545)		0.591*** (0.151)	0.344*** (0.0654)		0.506*** (0.149)	-0.585 (0.878)	0.393* (0.209)	-1.491 (10.83)			
Age	-0.528*** (0.108)			-0.740*** (0.122)		-0.310 (0.300)	-11.94* (5.307)	-0.167 (0.214)	-0.114 (3.136)			
Trade		0.402*** (0.126)					-0.0420 (0.352)					
R&D												0.126 (0.0907)
Employee²					0.218*** (0.0279)							0.230 (0.250)
Age²					-0.266*** (0.0558)							0.155 (0.125)
NSC 3					1.186*** (0.441)							
NSC 4					-0.117 (0.0948)							
Exit						-0.349 (0.340)	-5.439 (2.930)					
Software						0.0301 (0.0790)	-0.429 (0.431)			0.234** (0.0985)	0.152 (0.448)	
KIS						0.268** (0.110)	1.070** (0.461)		0 (0.466)	0.592*** (0.129)	0.890 (0.680)	
Capital (total)									1.000** (0.465)			
Constant	1.038*** (0.235)	-1.415 (1.165)	2.224** (0.865)	0.973*** (0.337)	1.119*** (0.310)	0.439 (0.720)	4.383 (3.889)			1.372** (0.630)	-0.736 (3.300)	3.480 (3.566)
Observations	1571	64	370	1,193	1571	227	17	341	26	352	23	175
R-squared	0.376	0.489	0.040	0.323	0.380	0.400	0.785			0.264	0.622	0.048
Number of firmid												46

Note: Robust standard errors in parentheses. *** p<0.01, ** p<0.05, * p<0.1

Legend: Ordinary Least Square (OLS). Olley and Pakes method (OP). Levinsohn and Petrin method (LP). Instrumental variable (IV).

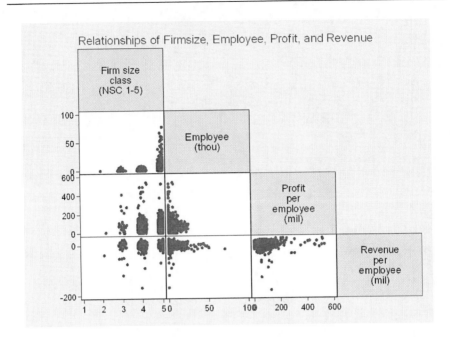

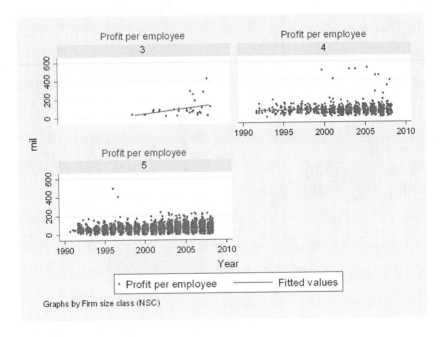

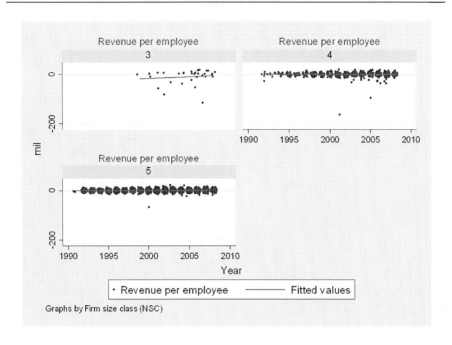

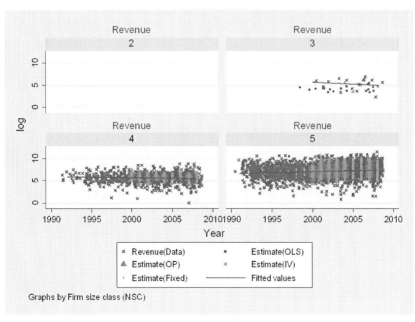

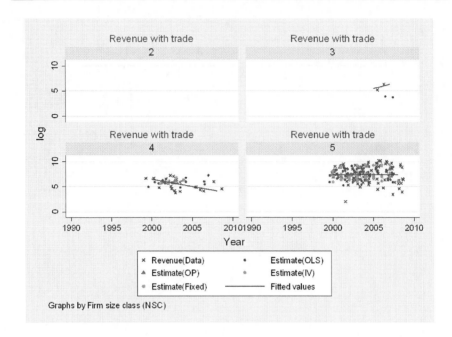

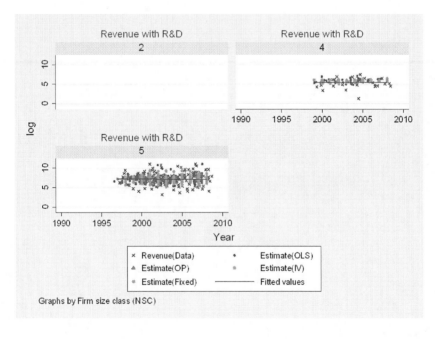

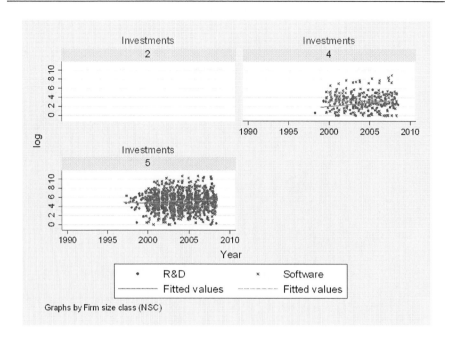

Graphs by Firm size class (NSC)

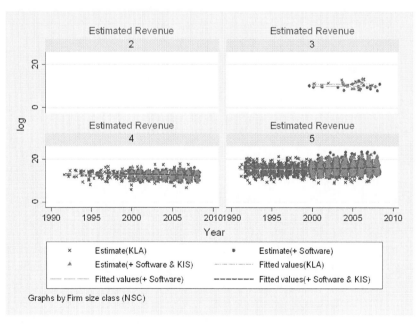

Graphs by Firm size class (NSC)

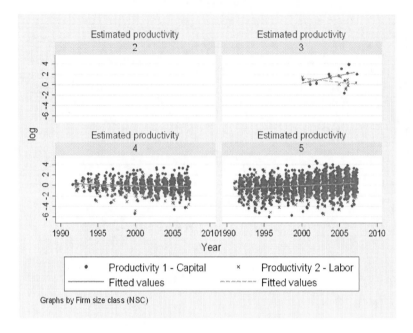

Figure 15. Summary of analysis for listed companies: Retail.

Analysis (2)
Type of firm: Unlisted
Time series: 2003-2009 (year)
Number of firms: 443
Number of observations: 4,374

Observation
According to Table 20, *employee* is statistically significant for OLS (Model 1-5). The coefficient is higher with NSC 1, which lowers as firms grow from NSC 1 to 5. According to Figure 16, productivity does not show an upward trend for capital, the labor productivity shows improvement in all firm size classes. According to the level of capital productivity, its gap between labor productivity is widest with NSC 1. The gap becomes smaller as firm grows large, and it widens slightly with NSC 5. The distribution of capital productivity becomes largest with NSC 4 and 5. This distribution may be the cause of the scattered revenues within the same size classes. Labor productivity with NSC 5 shows a higher level than the other size classes. Therefore, it may be proposed that when firm size is smaller, it is important to

invest into capital. At the same time, it is essential to focus on labor productivity growth when firms are still small.

Table 90. Summary of regression results
for unlisted companies: Retail

Retail

	(1)	(2)	(3)	(4)	(5)	(6)	(7)
REGRESSION	OLS	OLS: NSC 1	OLS: NSC 3	OLS: NSC 4	OLS: NSC 5	OLS: Size	Fixed effect
Independent Variables	Capital, Age, Employee	Capital, Employee	Capital, Employee	Capital, Employee	Capital, Employee	Capital, Employee, Employee^2, Age^2, NSC categorical dummies (1-5)	Capital, Age, Employee, Employee^2, Age^2
Capital	0.153***					0.230***	0.144***	-0.211*
	(0.0302)					(0.0345)	(0.0285)	(0.109)
Employee^2							0.400***	0.0305
							(0.0386)	(0.0678)
Age^2							-0.0920*	-0.00604
							(0.0491)	(0.0397)
NSC 2							-1.036*	
							(0.603)	
NSC 3							-1.368**	
							(0.549)	
NSC 4							-1.467**	
							(0.582)	
NSC 5							-1.836***	
							(0.640)	
Age	-0.181*							
	(0.105)							
Employee	0.635***	7.425**	1.174***	0.806***	0.707***		
	(0.0427)	(2.809)	(0.335)	(0.155)	(0.0882)		
Constant	1.089***	-10.96	-0.736	0.707	-0.219	1.761***	6.290***
	(0.272)	(5.611)	(1.347)	(0.863)	(0.576)	(0.558)	(1.027)
Observations	1047	7	110	420	492	1047	1047
R-squared	0.345	0.583	0.102	0.061	0.269	0.352	0.006
Number of firmid							349

Note: Robust standard errors in parentheses. *** p<0.01, ** p<0.05, * p<0.1

Legend: Ordinary Least Square (OLS).

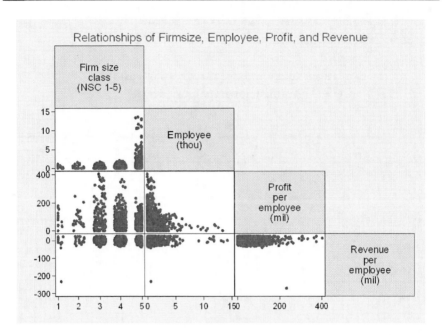

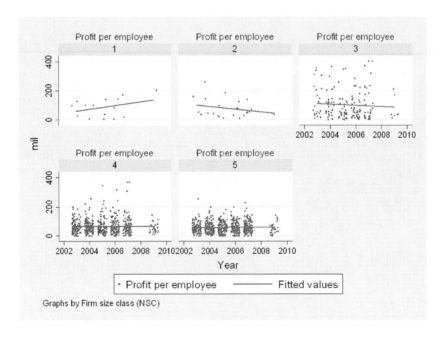

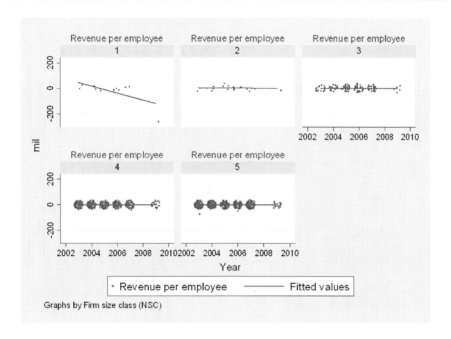

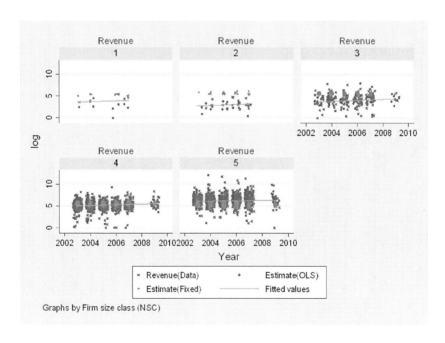

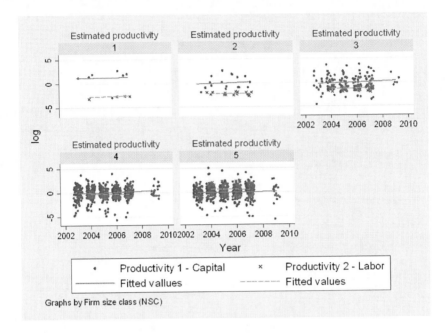

Figure 16. Summary of analysis for unlisted companies: Retail.

3.2.5. Industry: Service

Analysis (1)
Type of firm: Listed
Time series: 1991-2008 (year)
Number of firms: 525
Number of observations:

NSC	Freq.	Percent	Cum.
2	14	0.45	0.45
3	281	8.95	9.4
4	1,059	33.75	43.15
5	1,784	56.85	100
Total	3,138	100	

Observation

According to Table 21, *capital (tangibles)* and *capital (intangibles)* are important in the change in R2 followed by *R&D*. Table 22 shows that the sizes of firms look important for revenue as the statistics shows in terms of *employee*, and *employee*^{2} (Model 1, 2, 4 and 7). Firm size categorical dummies (*NSC*) show negative coefficients. At the same time, regression analyses show that there are not definitive variables in general. *Capital (tangibles), capital (intangibles), employee*, and/or *age* are statistically significant in most models. Looking at coefficients for employee in OLS (Model 1, 4, and 7), it shows that coefficients are highest for NSC 2. Therefore, it is effective for smaller firms to invest into labor to improve labor productivity earlier. When the impact of intermediate inputs is incorporated into analysis, *KIS* are found significant in instrumental variable (IV) model (Model 11 and 12). According to Figure 17, profit per employee and revenue per employee are both showing the same level for all size classes. The distribution of profit per employee and revenue per employee is very small and consistent throughout the dataset period. Productivity trend seems to be the same pattern. Revenue with trade is shrinking recently especially with NSC 4. The levels of R&D and software investment are on the same level for NSC 4 and 5. It seems effective for larger firms to continue to invest into R&D so that the revenue growth is maintained. As for the estimation of revenue, both *software* and *KIS* give positive impact on revenue for all sizes of firms. The combinatory impact of *KIS* and *software* gives a higher impact than the estimated revenue based on software only.

Table 101. Impact on R-squared for listed companies: Service

	(1)	(2)	(3)	(4)
Additional variables	Capital (tangibles)	Capital (intangibles)	R&D	Age
Observations	2498	2497	464	1821
R-squared	0.331	0.328	0.469	0.286
Change in R-squared	0.067	0.0635	0.0565	0.0042

Note: Dependent variable: Revenue.. Independent variable (default): Employee.

Table 112. Summary of regression results for listed companies: Service

Service

Model	(1)	(2)	(3)	(4)	(5)	(6)	(7)	(8)	(9)	(10)	(11)	(12)	(13)
REGRESSION	OLS	OLS: Trade	OLS: R&D	OLS: NSC 2	OLS: NSC 3	OLS: NSC 4	OLS: NSC 5	OLS: Size	OP	OP: Trade	IV	IV: Trade	Fixed Effect
Independent Variables	Capital (tangibles), Capital (intangibles), Employee, Age	For firms engaging in Trade: Capital (tangibles), Capital (intangibles), Employee, Age, Trade	For firms engaging in R&D: Capital (tangibles), Capital (intangibles), Employee, Age, Patent	Capital (tangibles), Capital (intangibles), Employee, Age, Patent	Capital (tangibles), Capital (intangibles), Employee, Age, Patent	Capital (tangibles), Capital (intangibles), Employee, Age, Patent	Capital (tangibles), Capital (intangibles), Employee, Age, Patent	For firms engaging in R&D (intangibles), Capital (intangibles), Employee, Age, Employee^2, Age^2, Patent, NSC categorical dummies (1-5)	Est, Age, Employee, KIS, R&D, Patent, Capital (tangibles), Capital (intangibles)	For firms engaging in Trade: Est, Age, Employee, KIS, R&D, Patent, Capital (tangibles), Capital (intangibles)	Instrumental variables (Software, KIS). Endogenous (Capital (tangibles), Capital (intangibles), Employee)	For firms engaging in Trade: Instrumental variables (Software, KIS). Endogenous variables (Capital (tangibles), Capital (intangibles), Employee)	For firms engaging in R&D: Capital (tangibles), Capital (intangibles), Employee, Capital (intangibles), Employee, Employee^2, Age^2
Capital (tangibles)	0.215*** (0.0166)	0.0947*** (0.0354)			0.100** (0.0489)	0.191*** (0.0253)	0.275*** (0.0243)	0.224*** (0.0166)	0.628 (0)	0.422 (0.335)			-0.0666 (0.146)
Capital (intangibles)	0.163*** (0.0173)	0.163*** (0.0337)	1.037*** (0.145)			0.122*** (0.0298)	0.194*** (0.0211)	0.144*** (0.0174)		0.0192 (0.200)			0.0478 (0.0473)
Employee^2								0.256*** (0.0229)					0.231** (0.115)
Age^2								-0.155*** (0.0548)					-0.193** (0.0952)
NSC 3								-0.728 (0.477)					
NSC 4								-1.331*** (0.482)					
NSC 5								-1.737*** (0.504)					
Employee	0.301*** (0.0264)	0.339*** (0.0706)		2.319** (0.821)	-1.097** (0.428)		0.477*** (0.0468)			0.183 (0.797)			
Age	-0.292** (0.119)	0.224*** (0.0489)								-0.297 (0.889)			
Trade										0.504 (0.462)			
Est										0.295 (0.600)			
Software									-2.776 (0)		-0.152 (0.183)	0.169 (0.272)	
KIS									1.171 (0)	-0.0176 (0.161)	1.523*** (0.382)	1.615*** (0.613)	
R&D									-0.650 (0)	-0.327* (0.163)			-0.0383 (0.0555)
Constant	1.865*** (0.175)	0.202 (0.320)	0.0859 (0.982)	-1.958 (2.109)	5.152*** (0.347)	3.725*** (0.221)	-0.392 (0.324)	2.064*** (0.481)	15.59 (0)	-0.936 (2.003)	-1.650 (1.707)	-3.815 (2.728)	4.091*** (1.247)
Observations	1819	481	14	6	129	582	1,102	1819	5	26	162	48	463
R-squared	0.399	0.484	0.725	0.516	0.062	0.135	0.427	0.412	1.000	0.784	-1.362	-0.487	0.061
Number of firmid													160

Note: Robust standard errors in parentheses. *** p<0.01, ** p<0.05, * p<0.1

Legend: Ordinary Least Square (OLS), Olley and Pakes method (OP), Instrumental variable (IV).

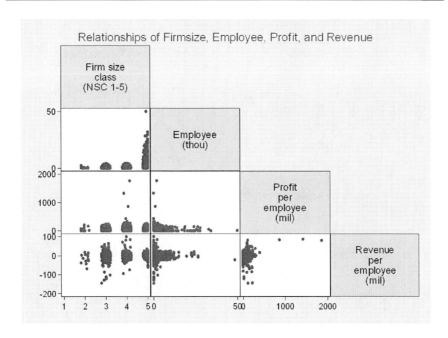

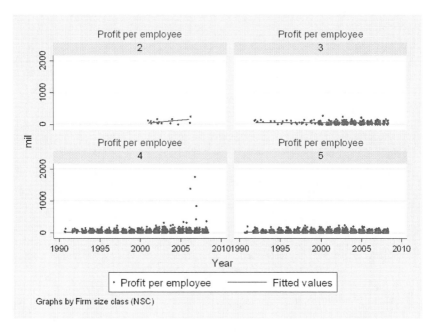

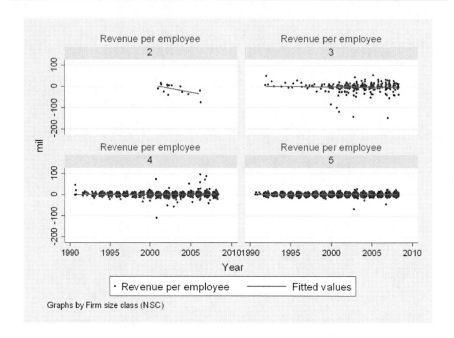

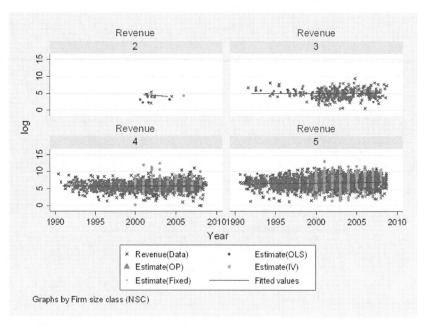

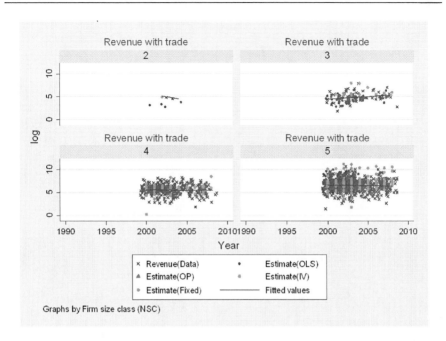

Graphs by Firm size class (NSC)

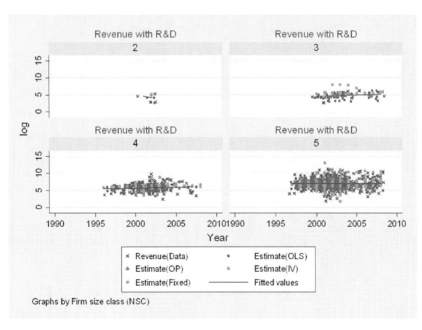

Graphs by Firm size class (NSC)

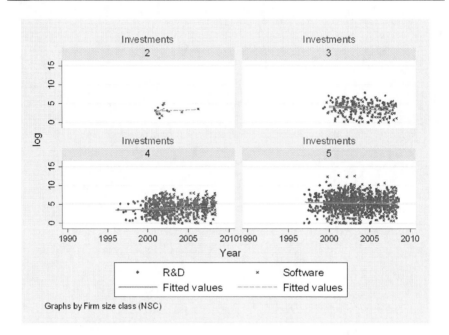

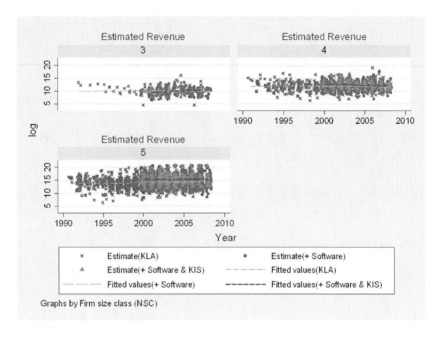

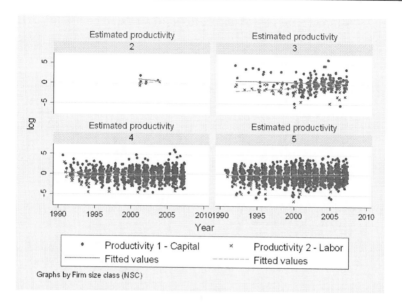

Figure 17. Summary of analysis for listed companies: Service.

Analysis (2)
Type of firm: Unlisted
Time series: 2003-2009 (year)
Number of firms: 1,280
Number of observations: 4,374

Observation

The number of firms in this analysis exceeds a thousand. Therefore, it is fairly a large-scale analysis. Particularly, service sector consists of a number of firms who are not listed. *Employee* seems to be an important independent variable for revenue according to Table 23 (Model 1, 4-6). According to Figure 18, the gap of revenue in each size class is very large. It widens as firm size grows, so as the trend of productivity. The trend of productivity, especially labor productivity, is distinguishing from the other sectors. Capital productivity is larger than labor productivity with NSC 1, however, labor productivity becomes higher for larger firm sizes. Coefficients for *capital* are lowering from OLS (Model 2-6). On the other hand, coefficient for *employee* is highest for OLS: NSC 3 (Model 4). It is suggested that it is important for smaller firms to improve labor productivity.

Table 123. Summary of regression results for unlisted companies: Service

	(1)	(2)	(3)	(4)	(5)	(6)	(7)	(8)
REGRESSION	OLS	OLS: NSC 1	OLS: NSC 2	OLS: NSC 3	OLS: NSC 4	OLS: NSC 5	OLS: Size	Fixed effect
Independent Variables	Capital, Age, Employee	Capital, Employee	Capital, Employee	Capital, Employee	Capital, Employee	Capital, Employee	Capital, Employee, Employee^2, Age^2, NSC categorical dummies (1-5)	Capital, Age, Employee, Employee^2, Age^2
Capital	0.363***	0.713***	0.510***	0.490***	0.302***	0.221***	0.358***	-0.000616
	(0.0188)	(0.135)	(0.0928)	(0.0334)	(0.0351)	(0.0279)	(0.0181)	(0.0545)
Employee^2							0.329***	0.113***
							(0.0229)	(0.0417)
Age^2							-0.241***	-0.210***
							(0.0379)	(0.0253)
NSC 2							-1.028***	
							(0.214)	
NSC 3							-0.911***	
							(0.202)	
NSC 4							-0.416*	
							(0.243)	
NSC 5							-0.555*	
							(0.300)	
Age	-0.488***							
	(0.0700)							
Employee	0.723***			1.157***	0.529***	0.613***		
	(0.0180)			(0.105)	(0.0933)	(0.0577)		
Constant	-0.295*	-0.281	0.0677	-3.489***	0.480	0.498	0.678***	4.085***
	(0.155)	(0.527)	(0.352)	(0.392)	(0.537)	(0.396)	(0.236)	(0.521)
Observations	3429	67	147	924	1239	1052	3429	3429
R-squared	0.526	0.301	0.172	0.327	0.080	0.190	0.536	0.034
Number of firmid								1115

Note: Robust standard errors in parentheses. *** p<0.01, ** p<0.05, * p<0.1
Legend: Ordinary Least Square (OLS).

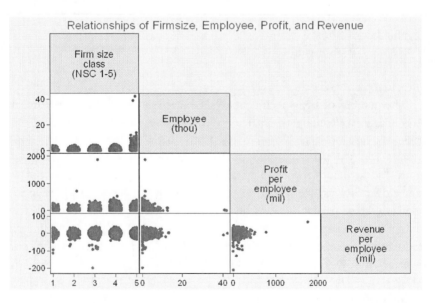

Relationships of Firmsize, Employee, Profit, and Revenue

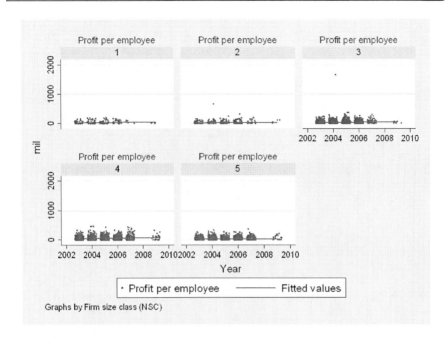

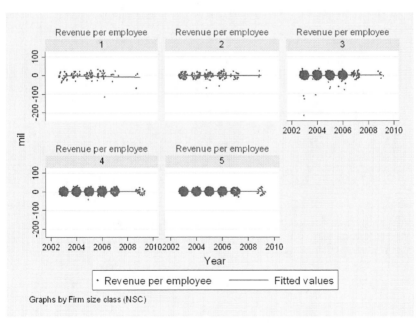

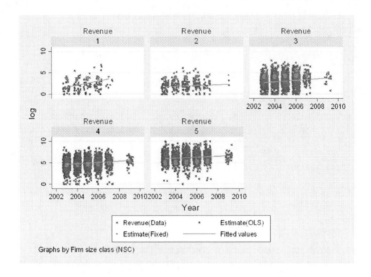

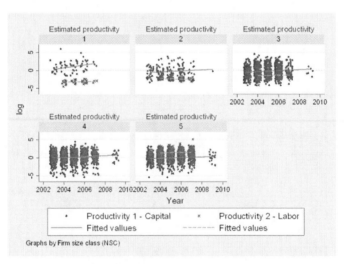

Figure 18. Summary of analysis for unlisted companies: Service.

3.2.6. Industry: Wholesale

Analysis (1)
Type of firm: Listed
Time series: 1991-2008 (year)
Number of firms: 432
Number of observations:

NSC	Freq.	Percent	Cum.
2	3	0.08	0.08
3	182	4.58	4.66
4	1,560	39.27	43.93
5	2,227	56.07	100
Total	3,972	100	

Observation

According to Table 24, *age* is the most important variable in terms of R2 although the level of impact is not large. Table 25 shows that *age* has negative coefficients in general (Model 1-4, and 7). From regression analyses, *capital (tangibles)*, *capital (intangibles)*, and *employee* are generally statistically significant (Model 1-6). With instrumental variable (IV) model only, *KIS* are found significant (Model 9). According to Figure 19, profit per employee shows a wide gap among firms particularly with NSC 5. On the other hand, revenue per employee shows a consistent pattern. Revenue with or without trade steadily grow in all sizes of firms. The trend of revenue for firms performing R&D is similar to the level of investment into *R&D*. Besides, *software* investment is higher than *R&D* expenditures. When *KIS* are incorporated into the estimation of revenue, the fitted value is slightly negative to data. Productivity of capital stays the same level across different firm sizes. The amount of investment into capital and labor seem to be the key for revenue growth. In this sector, it is supposed that the impact of *software* or *KIS* is small and the important factors for revenue growth are capital and labor.

Table 134. Impact on R-squared for listed companies: Wholesale

	(1)	(2)	(3)	(4)
Additional variables	Capital (tangibles)	Capital (intangibles)	R&D	Age
Observations	3237	3237	623	2309
R-squared	0.365	0.382	0.406	0.374
Change in R-squared	0.0023	0.0198	0.0153	0.0213

Note: Dependent variable: Revenue.. Independent variable (default): Employee.

Table 145. Summary of regression results for listed companies: Wholesale

Wholesale

Model REGRESSION	(1) OLS	(2) OLS: Trade	(3) OLS: R&D	(4) OLS: NSC 4	(5) OLS: NSC 5	(6) OLS: Size	(7) OP	(8) OP: Trade	(9) IV	(10) IV: Trade	(11) Fixed Effect
Independent Variables	Capital (tangibles), Capital (intangibles), Employee, Age	For firms engaging in Trade: Capital (tangibles), Capital (intangibles), Employee, Age, Trade	For firms engaging in R&D Capital (tangibles), Capital (intangibles), Employee, Age, Patent	Capital (tangibles), Capital (intangibles), Employee, Age, Patent	Capital (tangibles), Capital (intangibles), Employee, Age, Patent	For firms engaging in R&D Capital (intangibles), Employee, Age, Employee², Patent, Age², NSC categorical dummies (1-5)	Estt, Age, Employee, KIS, R&D, Patent, Capital (tangibles), Capital (intangibles)	For firms engaging in Trade: Estt, Age, Employee, KIS, R&D, Patent, Capital (tangibles), Capital (intangibles)	Instrumental variables (Software, KIS), Endogenous (Capital (tangibles), Capital (intangibles), Employee)	For firms engaging in Trade: Instrumental variables (Software, KIS), Endogenous (Capital (tangibles), Capital (intangibles), Employee)	For firms engaging in R&D: Capital (tangibles), Capital (intangibles), Employee, Employee², Age²
Capital (tangibles)	0.0747*** (0.0288)	0.181*** (0.0538)	0.631*** (0.153)	0.731** (0.312)	0.635*** (0.139)	0.0719*** (0.0244)	0.922 (0.457)	0.517** (0.241)			-0.0290 (0.147)
Capital (intangibles)	0.0806*** (0.0174)	0.0720* (0.0414)	0.327*** (0.0834)	0.212** (0.0987)	0.762*** (0.150)	0.0786*** (0.0173)	-1.412 (1.625)	0.0763 (0.0831)			0.0566 (0.0431)
Employee	0.601*** (0.0409)	0.460*** (0.0935)					-3.440 (1.633)	-0.211 (0.289)			
Age	-0.635*** (0.0862)	-0.908*** (0.196)	-1.516*** (0.496)	-1.550** (0.561)			-5.278* (1.828)	-0.880 (0.585)			
Trade		0.137*** (0.0322)									
Employee²						0.321*** (0.0237)		0.0446 (0.128)			0.224 (0.136)
Age²						-0.315*** (0.0456)					-0.110* (0.0571)
NSC 3						0.276 (0.173)					
NSC 4						0.0675 (0.0707)					
R&D							1.410 (1.232)	-0.0120 (0.127)			-0.0104 (0.0455)
Software							2.211 (1.210)		0.0141 (0.0695)	0.162 (0.116)	
Patent							0.470 (0.486)				
KIS							0.946 (0.718)	0.126 (0.0926)	0.669*** (0.116)	0.310 (0.346)	
Exit								0.497 (0.781)			
Constant	1.911*** (0.169)	0.853* (0.451)	-0.115 (1.148)	-0.167 (2.474)	-2.995** (1.210)	1.646*** (0.258)	10.25 (8.372)	2.740 (1.824)	2.714*** (0.448)	4.323*** (1.364)	3.920** (1.815)
Observations	2309	452	31	19	12	2309	12	61	472	135	623
R-squared	0.384	0.397	0.702	0.530	0.888	0.384	0.917	0.293	-0.164	-0.010	0.036
Number of firmid											143

Note: Robust standard errors in parentheses *** p<0.01, ** p<0.05, * p<0.1

Legend: Ordinary Least Square (OLS). Olley and Pakes method (OP). Instrumental variable (IV).

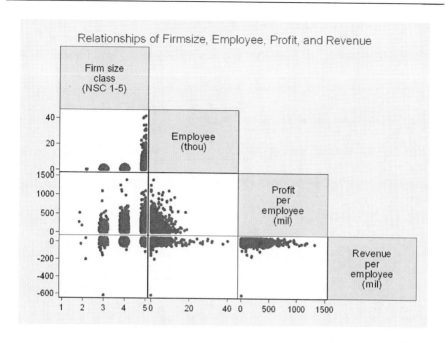

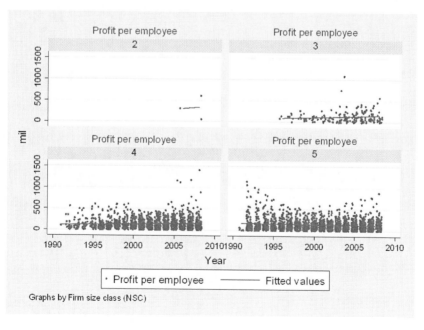

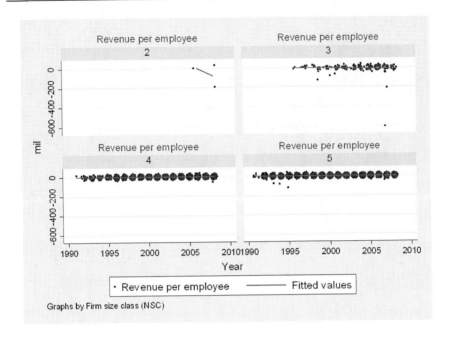

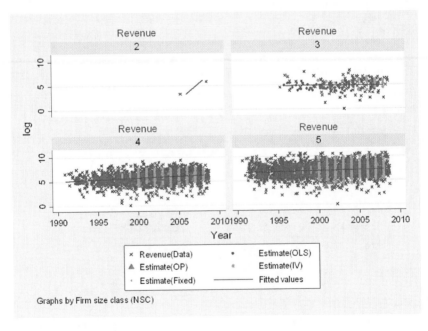

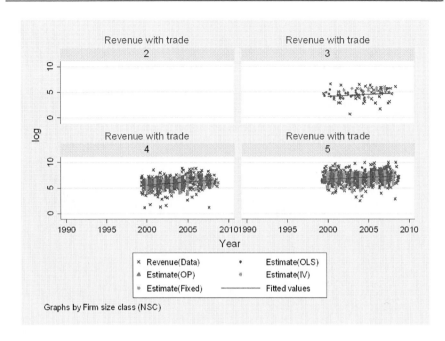

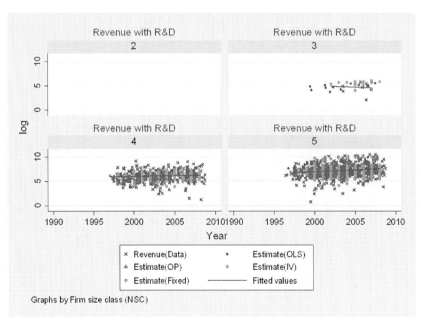

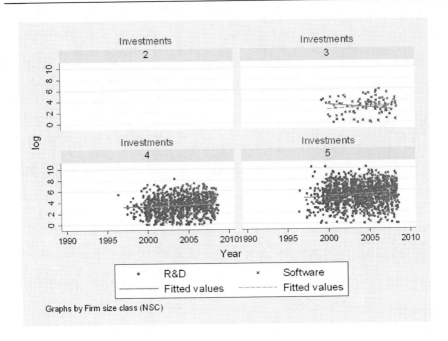

Graphs by Firm size class (NSC)

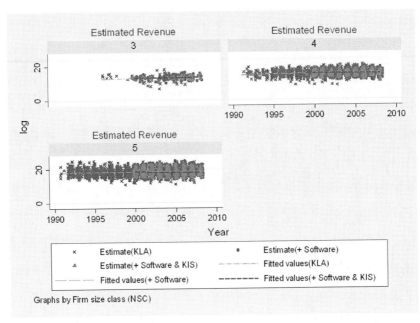

Graphs by Firm size class (NSC)

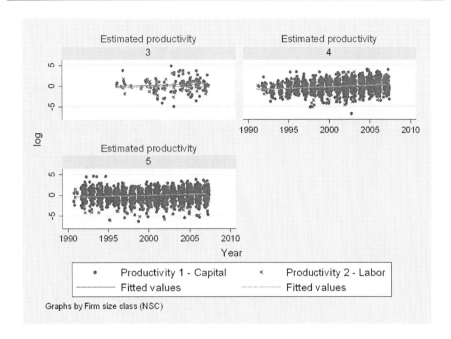

Figure 19. Summary of analysis for listed companies: Wholesale.

Analysis (2)
Type of firm: Unlisted
Time series: 2003-2009 (year)
Number of firms: 877
Number of observations: 3,175

Observation
According to Table 26, it is a consistent trend that *employee* is statistically significant with NSC 3 through NSC 5, in which coefficients are becoming large from NSC 3 to 5 in OLS regression (Model 1, and 3-6). *Capital* is also significant in all models, where coefficients are becoming small from NSC 1 to 5 in OLS regression (1-6). According to Figure 20, NSC 3 starts showing wider distribution of revenue among firms, which is maximized with NSC 4. For NSC 5, the distribution of revenue shrinks. It is suggestive to look at capital productivity trend. From NSC 3, the diversification of productivity starts to emerge. For NSC 5 the level of labor productivity exceeds that of capital productivity. For this sector, the role of capital and labor as well as their productivity seem to be important.

Yumiko Kinoshita

Table 156. Summary of regression results for unlisted companies: Wholesale

Wholesale

Model	(1)	(2)	(3)	(4)	(5)	(6)	(7)	(8)
REGRESSION	OLS	OLS: NSC 1	OLS: NSC 2	OLS: NSC 3	OLS: NSC 4	OLS: NSC 5	OLS: Size	Fixed effect
Independent Variables	Capital, Age, Employee	Capital, Employee	Capital, Employee	Capital, Employee	Capital, Employee	Capital, Employee	Capital, Employee, Employee^2, Age^2, NSC categorical dummies (1-5)	Capital, Age, Employee, Employee^2, Age^2
Capital	0.261***	0.900***	0.704*	0.373***	0.240***	0.161***	0.262***	-0.0998
	(0.0238)	(0.294)	(0.402)	(0.0476)	(0.0246)	(0.0499)	(0.0197)	(0.0893)
Employee^2							0.340***	0.125**
							(0.0252)	(0.0593)
Age^2							-0.274***	-0.359***
							(0.0299)	(0.0219)
NSC 2							0.173	
							(0.306)	
NSC 3							0.757***	
							(0.257)	
NSC 4							0.614**	
							(0.287)	
NSC 5							0.490	
							(0.339)	
Age	-0.558***							
	(0.0623)							
Employee	0.655***	-3.321***		0.505***	0.710***	0.823***		
	(0.0287)	(1.065)		(0.140)	(0.0589)	(0.131)		
Constant	1.423***	4.939***	-0.0292	0.786	0.389	0.00647	0.653**	5.770***
	(0.172)	(1.357)	(1.718)	(0.575)	(0.335)	(0.811)	(0.263)	(0.786)
Observations	2679	26	32	559	1701	361	2679	2679
R-squared	0.360	0.320	0.093	0.140	0.133	0.181	0.365	0.128
Number of firmid								795

Note: Robust standard errors in parentheses. *** p<0.01, ** p<0.05, * p<0.1

Legend: Ordinary Least Square (OLS).

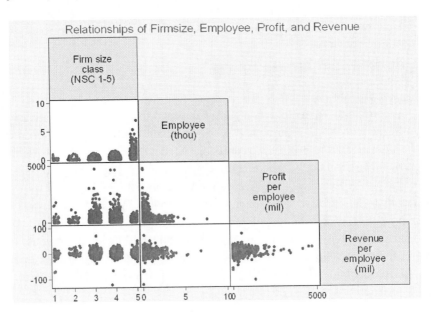

Relationships of Firmsize, Employee, Profit, and Revenue

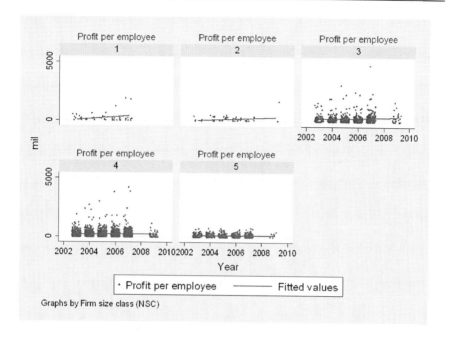

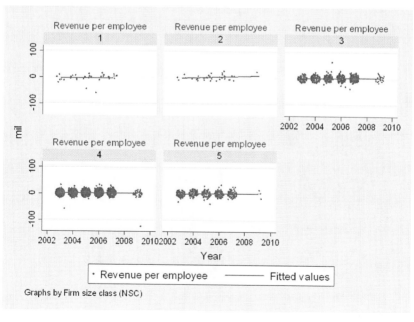

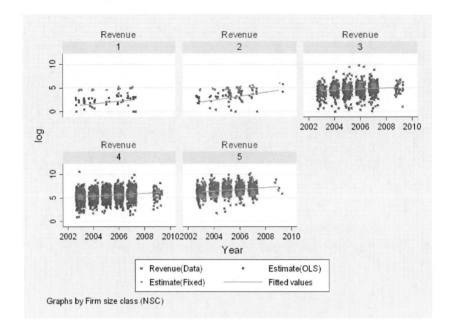

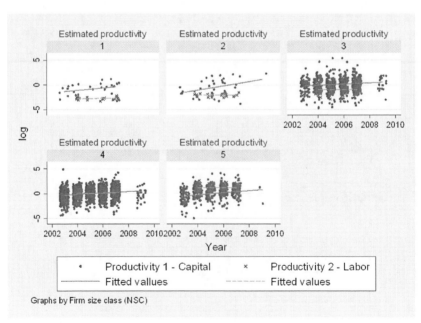

Figure 20. Summary of analysis for unlisted companies: Wholesale.

3.3. RESULT OF MACROECONOMIC ANALYSIS

In this section, the macroeconomic trend of the Japanese economy is observed first. Then, gross output is estimated in both conventional models as well as the models specifically designed in this chapter so that we can examine the impact of service inputs, ICT investment and the parameter (ρ) on macro economy.

First of all, Source: Figures are created based on data obtained from EU KLEMS database, Japan, November 2009 release. Data period is 1974-2006.

Figure 21 shows that GDP had grown until early 1990s and has entered a leveled ground since then. Japan has exhibited a negative growth four times from 1993 to 2008. ICT capital formation also tends to be on a leveled ground from the 1990s. The ratio of ICT capital to total assets shows an increase until 1990 and between mid 1990s to year 2000. After 2000, it shows a continuous decline. Meanwhile, the ratio of consumption of ICT is steadily growing and outpaces the growth rate of ICT capital. That of ICT capital also shows a linear and positive upward trend to GDP although the rate of increase is slower than the total capital. In line with this trend, the use of intermediate services is steadily increasing over the dataset period so as its share in total intermediaries.

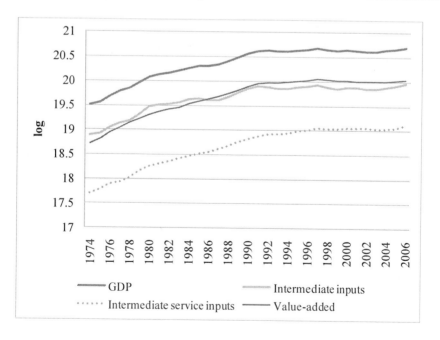

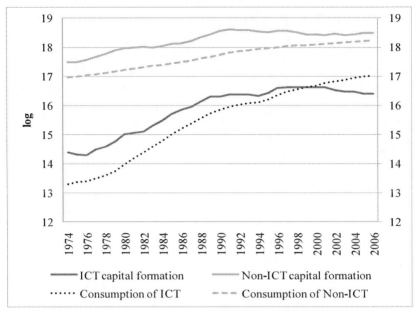

Source: Figures are created based on data obtained from EU KLEMS database, Japan,
    November 2009 release. Data period is 1974-2006.

Figure 21. Japan's macroeconomic trend.

According to the estimation of gross output in the following figure, the
first methodology for the estimation (K, L, and ICT investment) shows the
second closest fit to the actual GDP trend. One of the standard approaches
(lagged value added and lagged ICT investment) and the model specifically
designed for this chapter (service inputs in K, and service productivity) yield
similar curves. The last one (service intermediate inputs in K, C and lagged
ICT investment) shows the best fit to the actual GDP curve. Therefore, the
curve of using productivity (service intermediate inputs, and service
productivity) and the last one (service intermediate inputs, C and lagged ICT
investment) are understood as valid estimation models. They are chosen for
further analysis in simulation scenarios.

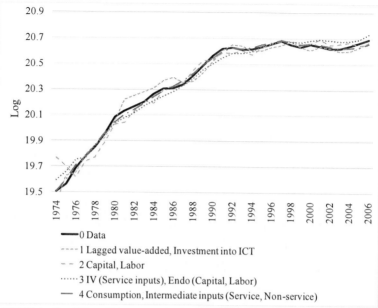

Note: 'GDP' in the title refers to nominal gross output. Data are taken directly from
   EU KLEMS database, which correspond to '0 Data.' GDP is estimated in a
   regression model with K and L as independent variables. 'Lagged value-added,
   Investment into ICT' is the estimation based on lagged value added and the
   amount of investment into ICT. 'IV (Service inputs), Endo (Capital, Labor)' is
   related to the definition of K in Eq.(2.4.4), and L in Eq.(2.4.5), which reflect the
   parameter 'ρ' obtained from Eq.(2.3.15). 'Consumption, Intermediate inputs
   (Service, Non-service) reflect the impact of the parameter 'ρ' in C and the use of
   intermediate inputs. Therefore, the parameter is reflected in K and L in the third,
   and C in the forth models respectively.
Source: The figure is author's calculations based on data obtained from EU KLEMS
   database, Japan, November 2009 release. Data period is 1974-2006.

Figure 22. Estimated GDP.

Source: The figure is created based on data obtained from EU KLEMS
database, Japan, November 2009 release. Data period is 1974-2006. Data on
GDP is directly taken from the source. Detrended GDP is author's calculation.

   Figure 23 shows the difference of estimated GDP to actual GDP
(estimation over real value). The trend curve picks up first. After some
fluctuations, it drops sharply and then steadily shows an upward trend. This

overall trend should be understood coupled with the trend of detrended GDP[1]. The detrended GDP shows a trend of gross output with the impact of productivity multiplied by laborforce subtracted so that the impact of capital (K) becomes more clear. According to the figure, the detrended GDP curve continues to decline from early 1990s, and the gap between the actual GDP and the detrended one is widening. It is assumed that the positive effect of productivity and labor force on GDP is rising contrary to the impact of capital formation. The estimation in Source: The figure is created based on data obtained from EU KLEMS database, Japan, November 2009 release. Data period is 1974-2006. Data on GDP is directly taken from the source. Detrended GDP is author's calculation.

Figure 23 shows the trend of GDP and the degree of impacts derived from ICT capital formation; however, it is limited to examine the behavior of service economy i.e. purchased knowledge services and knowledge spillover.

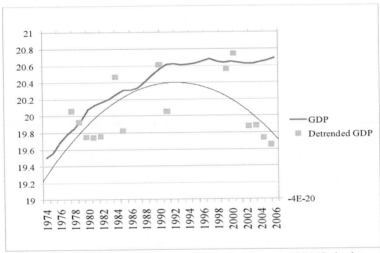

Source: The figure is created based on data obtained from EU KLEMS database, Japan, November 2009 release. Data period is 1974-2006. Data on GDP is directly taken from the source. Detrended GDP is author's calculation.

Figure 23. Impact of Productivity.

---

[1] Detrended GDP is obtained from $y_t \equiv \dfrac{Y_t}{A_t^{1-\theta} N_t}$ according to Basu, S., Fernald, J. & Kimball, M. (2006).

In line with these observations, the 3rd and 4th model are used for further analysis in Figure 24. In particular, according to the (a)'s GDP curve, the scenario of increasing service intermediate inputs by 120% shows a positive impact on GDP, whose degree of impact is modest compared to the scenario of decreasing service inputs by 20% and increasing ICT capital by 20%. The latter scenario yields a sharper curve with more distinctive and faster diminishing return than the former scenario. The former scenario gives not as a strong and positive impact on GDP as the latter scenario does through the formation of capital and the use of labor, however, the positive impact of the former lasts longer than the latter scenario. The scenario of increasing service intermediate by 20% and reducing ICT capital by 20% shows a negative impact first in terms of the effect on consumption, and picks up afterword. On the other hand, the scenario of decreasing service inputs by 20% and increasing ICT capital by 20% starts to give a positive impact on GDP through consumption more slowly than the former scenario although its impact on GDP is stronger than the former.

According to (a) and (b)'s estimation results in Figure 24, the increase of service inputs gives positive effect on the trend of service productivity, and thus on the entire economy. Comparing (a) and (c) in Figure 24 suggests that the scenario of increasing service by 130% and the scenario of reducing service intermediate inputs by 20% and increasing ICT capital formation by 20% gives almost the same level of positive impact on GDP. Then, according to (b), the positive upward impact on GDP becomes weaker if ICT capital formation is reduced.

Besides, it is also proved that the growth trend of the economy would be negatively affected if ICT consumption only is promoted according to the trend of (d). As previously mentioned, the consumption of ICT has been growing at a faster pace than that of ICT capital formation. This situation is suggesting that an expansionary policy targeting the increase of final demand in ICT is not effective and Japan needs to be aware of the co-evolving process of ICT capital formation and the utilization of service intermediaries.

These results show that the service inputs need to be supported by ICT capital formation, and that a possible expansionary policy for promoting ICT consumption does not yield a positive result for the overall economy by itself according to (d)'s result. Furthermore, the scenario of increasing service intermediate inputs by 30% gives a positive impact on GDP through the increase of consumption, and its impact becomes modest for the scenario of increasing service intermediate inputs by 20% and reducing ICT capital formation by 20% according to (e) and (f)'s results. According to (f), service intermediate inputs support consumption even if ICT capital is decreased. Although the increase in service intermediaries gives not a sharp impact as the increase in ICT capital, service intermediaries take a role as moderator of total economic fluctuations and smoothes out the trend curve. The negative impact on ICT capital, then, becomes smaller.

Overall, it is suggested that a combination of the use of ICT capital and service intermediaries should be appropriately considered for the current and future economy. As for the service productivity, the impact of purchased external knowledge and knowledge spillover are relatively weaker compared to the internal investment into knowledge (i.e. R&D). Therefore, it is suggested that appropriate measures should be taken for the future economic growth to enhance the use of external expertise knowledge and promote its spillover.

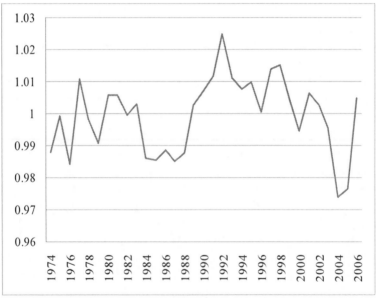

(a) Service intermediate inputs (130%) based on the 3rd model
(Service inputs, Capital, Labor)

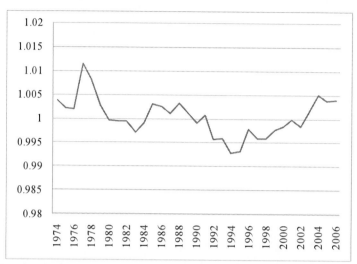

(b) Service intermediate inputs (120%) and ICT capital formation (80%)
based on the 3rd model (Service inputs, Capital, Labor)

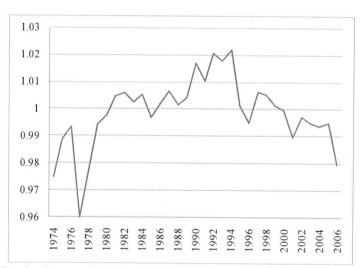

(c) Service intermediate inputs (80%) and ICT capital formation (120%)
based on the 3rd model (Service inputs, Capital, Labor)

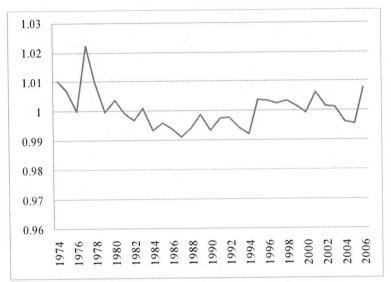

(d) ICT consumption (130%) based on the 3rd model
(Service inputs, Capital, Labor)

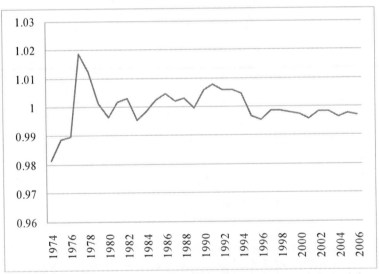

(e) Service intermediate inputs (130%) based on the 4th model
(Consumption, Intermediate inputs (Service, Non-service))

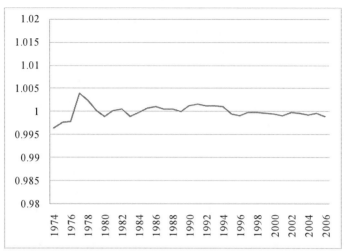

(f) Service intermediate inputs (120%) and ICT capital formation (80%) based on the 4th model (Consumption, Intermediate inputs (Service, Non-service))

Note: The solid lines show the difference in percentage from the original GDP data.
Source: The figures are author's caluculations based on data obtained from EU KLEMS database, Japan, November 2009 release. Data period is 1974-2006.

Figure 24. Impacts on GDP – Individual Views.

3.4. SUMMARY

As an overview of the microeconomic analyses, it is suggested that it is important to observe service industries at sectoral level so that the distribution of revenue per employee can be examined in detail in relation to productivity. This chapter focuses on this micro-level analysis first so that it is linked to broader perspectives on macro economy later. It is pointed out that the ratio of SMEs in Japan's service sectors are decreasing while that of the other countries are increasing. The ratio of SMEs in Japan's industries is higher than that of the other countries; however, contrary to the other countries, the number of SMEs is decreasing. This is a unique characteristic pertaining to Japan. It is important to be reminded of this fact when we investigate the service sectors from the viewpoint of business sizes.

Based on the regression analyses that aim at revealing structural aspects for the growth of productivity for the service sectors, it is assumed, first of all, that productivity in the service sectors should be considered in a way, which is expressed in the change of Pareto distribution curve. For these reasons, it is important to utilize the firm size distributions and the shift of the productivity curve within each sector so that revenue in the service sectors should reach an optimal level. If it is safe to say that the curve represents the revenue distribution well enough as a proxy, then, the fact that the number of SMEs in Japan is decreasing means that Japan is not being able to utilize the positive effect of the shift of productivity distribution among firm sizes. It is suggested that this trend can be a cause of the current slower growth of the entire service sectors in Japan. Therefore, it is proposed that there is the need for promoting SMEs in Japan by utilizing service inputs in addition to IT infrastructure.

Analyses are performed at sectoral level for service sectors in addition to a manufacturing sector so that a good comparison can be made to find general trends for the service sectors. In general, when *capital (intangibles)* comes first in terms of the impact on R2, *patent* and *software* are important variables for the determination of revenue. In some sectors, the diminishing returns in terms of size class (not in terms of duration of operation) for capital productivity can be observed very clearly. For such sectors, the improvement of revenue is observed among small to medium-sized firms as long as they shift their focus on human resources (*employee*). Then, *KIS* give positive impacts on revenue even after capital productivity is lowered among large firms. When the level of software investment is higher than that of R&D, it is suggestive that the level of software investment is related to the impact coming from *KIS*. In some cases, capital productivity is slightly higher than labor productivity although the gap is very small. In addition, the regression analyses show diversified results, in which significant independent variables are not consistent. Either the investment trend or the environment to utilize the investment is not distinctive from the other sectors, causing a lack of factors for revenue improvement.

This section addresses the issue of service innovation and the creation of structured knowledge utilizing technologies, namely IT. As we have witnessed recently in the financial crisis, the direction of future IT services and networking technologies has a huge impact on the course of the entire service sector to take for years ahead. As mentioned, the discussion on the size of firms is important in terms of finding the optimal scale of investment into IT system, and designing innovation policies. The hypothesis is the shift of Pareto curve among service sectors represented by the variations of profit structures by firm size. A thorough analysis on the relationship between firm size and turnover in the service sector has rarely been seen in previous literatures. In particular, this analysis encompasses the impact of R&D in services, which is, by itself, a new topic for empirical analyses.

The productivity is derived from the micro-level analysis, which is fed into the macro-level analysis so that the growth of the entire economy is analyzed from the perspective of service sectors. The impact of ICT capital and service inputs to macro economy is also clarified. According to the result, the impact of an increase in service inputs is exhibited in a slower and moderate curve than that of ICT capital. ICT capital gives a stronger impact and follows a sharper diminishing return. Service intermediaries take a role as moderator of economic fluctuations. The combination of the use of ICT capital and service intermediaries should be appropriately considered for the current and future economy. It is suggested that appropriate measures should be taken to enhance the use of external expertise knowledge and promote its spillover for the future economic growth.

Chapter 5

CONCLUSION

In today's economy, the service sectors consist 70-75% of the economy in most advanced countries although we find that there is less empirical and statistical studies performed with regard to the service sector than manufacturing. Starting in the 1970s by Fuchs (1965), Hill (1977), Sasser, Olsen, and Wyckoff (1978), and Grönroos, et al. (Grönroos, 1990, 1999; Grönroos & Ojasalo, 2004), the characteristics of the service sector has been investigated. Service is defined as 'a change in condition or state of an economic entity (or thing) caused by another' (Hill, 1977). In general, service is characterized by intangibility and inseparatability. Moreover, as mentioned above, various services are serving as a facilitator of innovation process within and outside the sector (Wolfl, 2005).

Various statistical issues gather attention, one of which is how we measure real value added and productivity of service sectors. More recently, Jensen, et al. (2005), Amiti and Wei (2005), Triplett and Bosworth (2004), and Diewert, et al. (2009) are articulating the issues of deflator to measure the output of services with more accuracy. Atkinson (2009) has analyzed public services to investigate an appropriate deflator while Hartwig (2008) focuses on financial industries to analyze productivity. However, the number of empirical studies is very limited for the service sectors. In addition, the productivity of the service sector has not been identified clearly in relation to the growth of the service sector.

As previously explained, the impact of capital input, labor input and productivity varies widely in each service sector. However, there are common aspects that IT stock and high skill workers tend to allow the turnover per employee to become preferable for growing firms. It is important to articulate the importance of firm size variations, leading to the variations of profit structure in the service sector. The introduction of IT could connect markets, which used to be separated, and promote international trade. Local markets may face fierce competition against multinational enterprises, which may eventually lead them to lose their markets. The use of knowledge, either heterogeneous or expertise, to link these segmented markets is a tool to create new services and build up knowledge. This aspect must be carefully examined to allow for an optimal growth for the service sector.

As Krugman (1989), Melitz (2005; 2003) and Chaney (2008) argued, the issue of substitution is important to understand the effect of locality, elasticity of substitution of products, and expertise of knowledge when we think of the issue of trade either inter-nationally or inter-regionally. These aspects must be investigated in relation to the impact of IT stock and worker's skill composition so that the optimal growth path for the service sector should be clarified. It is necessary to focus on maintaining competitiveness for some locally-traded services while it is important to invest into innovative activities to increase knowledge expertise and gain competitive edge in the global market.

Taking this connection of technological and knowledge innovation into consideration, Cobb-Douglas function is used for the empirical analyses. The empirical analyses consist a firm-level analysis for both listed companies and unlisted companies, and macro economy. The first focus in the empirical analyses is the impact of firm size variations on revenue and productivity. The second point is the role of R&D. The third point is the use of software and KIS. The fourth point is the efficiency for the service sector in terms of the use and creation of knowledge. The impact of trade is also tested. To verify all these points, various regression models are experimentally used. The highlight of these analyses is, first of all, the incorporation of function, which estimates the production function in the presence of selection bias and simultaneity by using the three-stage algorithm described in Olley and Pakes (1996). The second highlight is the use of Levinsohn and Petrin (2003) model, which estimates production functions using intermediate inputs to control for unobservable productivity shocks.

According to the firm-level analysis for the service sector, intangibles are relevant to how effective KIS are in terms of the revenue growth. The balance of tangibles and intangibles, which is represented in the distribution of capital productivity, seems to give an important impact on the revenue trend in each size class and sector. There is an optimal firm size in each type of investment into R&D and software. The balance of R&D investment and how long a firm continues to operate is another key for a successful turnover growth. These observations can be an explanation of the stagnation of productivity in the entire service sector, and the structural factors that suggest the direction for future growth of the service sector. These analytical frameworks can be applied to other countries for investigating future economic trends and appropriate policies.

As for the macro economic analysis, both the estimated productivity in the firm-level analysis and the productivity taken from official statistics are comparatively reviewed to check biases in the test procedures and to observe how the estimated productivity in the service sector yields a different curve in the context of the entire macro economy. By doing so, the impact of intermediate service inputs is addressed in relation to the formation and consumption of ICT capital. According to the result of simulations, the increase in service intermediaries gives not a large impact as ICT capital does although service intermediaries take a role as moderator of total economic fluctuations and smoothen out the trend curve. The diminishing return observed with ICT capital, then, can be alleviated by the co-investment into ICT and service. Therefore, the combination of the use of ICT capital and service intermediaries should be appropriately considered for the current and future economy.

As previously explained, the level of capital, labor and productivity varies widely in each service sector. Based on the review on major statistics and previous literatures, it is proposed to address the importance of firm size distributions, leading to the variations of profit structure in the service sector. Another important point is the different trend that is the growth of the service sector promoted by the introduction of IT and expertise knowledge services, by either internally, externally, or with public support, that aims to improve productivity. In this regard, it is articulated that KIS have a special role to play for facilitating innovation. The other point that gathers attention in a recent few years is the impact of service R&D, which is performed to increase knowledge expertise and gain competitiveness in a global market. In line with these trends, this research aims at arguing economic growth models based on that innovation in the service sector is promoted and transformed with the appropriate combination of IT and services.

ACKNOWLEDGMENT

Professor Osamu Sudoh, the University of Tokyo, Professor Hideyuki Tanaka, and Associate Professor Reiko Gotoh, Ibaragi University have offered deep insights on the concept of service innovation and its measurement. I appreciate fully for their insights particularly Professor Sudoh as he has provided theoretical foundation on network economy and the role of IT in the society and economy as well as policy and technical perspectives on public IT services in Japan. I owe so much for constructing the idea, finding methodologies, and drawing good implications for today's service economy. Associate Professor, Syungo Sakaki, Tokyo Institute of Technology, has offered important inputs regarding analysis methodology and the selection of data. I appreciate the feedback offered by Associate Professor Hiroshi Ohashi, the University of Tokyo, with regard to the measurement method of innovation and productivity. I acknowledge information on international trade in services from Associate Professor Yukiko Itoh, Tokyo Gakugei University as very useful. In addition, Assistant Professor Yun Jeong Choi, the University of Tokyo, was supporting data collection and offered feedback on measuring the impact on R&D. The author is responsible for any possible mistake in this chapter.

REFERENCES

Acemoglu, D., Aghion, P., Lelarge, C., Van Reenen, J. & Zilibotti, F. (2007). Technology, Information, and the Decentralization of the Firm. *Quarterly Journal of Economics, 122(4)*, 1759-1799.

Ackerberg, D., Benkard, L. C., Berry, S. & Pakes, A. (2007). Econometric Tools for Analyzing Market Outcomes. In J. J. Heckman, & E. E. Leamer (Eds.), *Handbook of Econometrics* (Vol 6A, pp. 4171-4276): Elsevier.

Acs, Z. J., & Audretsch, D. B. (1988). Innovation in Large and Small Firms - An Empirical Analysis. *American Economic Review, 78(4)*, 678-690.

Amiti, M., & Wei, S. J. (2005). Fear of Service Outsourcing -Is It Justified? *Economic Policy, 20(42)*, 308-347.

Andrews, D. W. K., & Stock, J. H. (2007). Testing with Many Weak Instruments. *Journal of Econometrics, 138,* 24-46.

Aoki, M. (2001). *Toward a Comparative Institutional Analysis*: The MIT Press.

Arellano, M. (1989). A Note on the Anderson-Hsiao Estimator for Panel Data. *Econometrics Letters, 31,* 337-341.

Arellano, M., Honoré, B., Heckman, J. J., & Leamer, E. E. (2001). Panel Data Models: Some Recent Developments In J. J. Heckman, & E. E. Leamer (Eds.), *Handbook of Econometrics* (Vol 5, pp. 3229-3296): Elsevier.

Asheim, B. T., & Gertler, M. S. (2005). The Geography of Innovation: Regional Innovation Systems. In J. Fagerberg, D. C. Mowery & R. R. Nelson (Eds.), *The Oxford Handbook of Innovation* (pp. 291-317): Oxford University Press.

Atkinson, A. B. (2009). *The Atkinson Review –The Measurement of Government Outputs for the National Accounts*: Palgrave Macmillan.

Atkinson, R. D., & Castro, D. D. (2008). Digital Quality of Life - Understanding the Personal & Social Benefits of the Information Technology Revolution: Information Technology and Innovation Foundation.http://www.itif.org/publications/digital-quality-life-understanding-benefits-it-revolution

Atkinson, R. D., & Wial, H. (2008). Boosting Productivity, Innovation, and Growth Through a National Innovation Foundation: Brookings and Information Technology & Innovation Foundation. http://www.itif.org/files/NIF.pdf

Audretsch, D. B., & Feldman, M. P. (1996). R&D Spillovers and the Geography of Innovation and Production. *American Economic Review, 86(3)*, 630-640.

Australian Bureau of Statistics. Characteristics of Small Business Survey. http://www.abs.gov.au/AUSSTATS/abs@.nsf/0/E49E3B4DC   3595 C92CA2568A900139377?OpenDocument

Austrian Institute for SME Research. Structural database. http://www.kmuforschung.ac.at/EN/index.htm

Aw, B. Y., Roberts, M. J., & Xu, D. Y. (2008). R&D Investments, Exporting, and the Evolution of Firm Productivity. *American Economic Review, 98(2)*, 451-456.

Bajari, P., Benkard, C. L., & Levin, J. (2007). Estimating Dynamic Models of Imperfect Competition. *Econometrica, 75(5)*, 1331-1370.

Barras, R. (1986). Towards a Theory of Innovation in Services. *Research Policy, 15(4)*, 161-173.

Basu, S., & Fernald, J. (2006). Information and Communications Technology as a General-Purpose Technology -Evidence from U.S Industry Data. *German Economic Review, 8(2)*, 146-173.

Basu, S., Fernald, J. & Kimball, M. (2006) Are Technology Improvements Contractionary? *American Economic Review, 96(5)*, 1418-1448.

Baum, C. F., Schaffer, M. E., & Stillman, S. (2003). Instrumental Variables and GMM -Estimation and Testing. *The Stata Journal, 3(1)*, 1-31.

Bayona, C., García-Marco, T., & Huerta, E. (2001). Firms' Motivations for Cooperative R&D -An Empirical Analysis of Spanish Firms. *Research Policy, 30(8)*, 1289-1307.

Bayoumi, T., Coe, D. T., & Helpman, E. (1999). R&D Spillovers and Global Growth. *Journal of International Economics, 47(2)*, 399-428.

Belderbos, R., Carree, M., Diederen, B., Lokshin, B., & Veugelers, R. (2004). Heterogeneity in R&D Cooperation Strategies. *International Journal of Industrial Organization, 22(8-9)*, 1237-1263.

Bernard, A. B., Eaton, J., Jensen, J. B., & Kortum, S. (2003). Plants and Productivity in International Trade. *American Economic Review, 93(4)*, 1268-1290.

Bernstein, J. I., & Mamuneas, T. P. (2006). R&D Depreciation, Stocks, User Costs and Productivity Growth for US R&D Intensive Industries. *Structural Change and Economic Dynamics, 17(1)*, 70-98.

Besanko, D., & Doraszelski, U. (2004). Capacity Dynamics and Endogenous Asymmetries in Firm Size. *RAND Journal of Economics, 35(1)*, 23-49.

Bloom, N. (2007). Uncertainty and the Dynamics of R&D. *American Economic Review, 97(2)*, 250-255.

Borresen, P. L. (2007). OIOUBL -Case Study of How to Implement a Nationwide Procurement Standard. Paper presented at OASIS Symposium, San Diego, California.

Bosworth, B. P., & Triplett, J. E. (2007). Is the 21st Century Productivity Expansion Still in Services? And What Should Be Done About It? National Bureau of Economic Research and Conference on Research in Income and Wealth. http://www.brookings.edu/~/media/ Files/rc/papers/ 2007/01_productivity_bosworth/01_productivity_bosworth.pdf

Bourguignon, F., & Pereira da Silva L. A., (2003). *The Impact of Economic Policies on Poverty and Income Distribution*: The World Bank and Oxford University Press.

Bresnahan, T. F., Brynjolfsson, E., & Hitt, L. M. (2002). Information Technology, Workplace Organization, and the Demand for Skilled Labor: Firm-Level Evidence. *Quarterly Journal of Economics, 117(1)*, 339-376.

Brun, M. H., & Lanng, C. (2006). Reducing barriers for e-business in SME's through an open service oriented infrastructure. Paper presented at the 8th International Conference on Electronic Commerce, 403-410.

Bryson, J. R., Daniels, P. W., & Warf, B. (2004). *Service Worlds*: Routledge.

Buyya, R., Yeo, C. C., & Venugopal, S. (2008). Market-oriented Cloud Computing: Vision, Hype, and Reality for Delivering IT Services as Computing Utilities. Paper presented at the 10th IEEE International Conference on High Performance Computing and Communications, 5-13.

Cainelli, G., Evangelista, R., & Savona, M. (2006). Innovation and Economic Performance in Services -A Firm-level Analysis. *Cambridge Journal of Economics, 30*, 435-458.

Canova, F. (2007). Dynamic Macro Panels. In F. Canova (Ed.), *Methods for Applied Macroeconomic Research* (pp.288-324): Princeton University Press.

Carree, M. A. & Thurik, A. R. (1998). Small Firms and Economic Growth in Europe. *Atlantic Economic Journal, 26,* 137-146.

Carree, M. A., & Thurik, A. R. (2000). Industrial Structure and Economic Growth. In D. B. Audretsch & A. R. Thurik (Eds.), *Innovation, Industry Evolution, and Economic Growth* (pp. 86-110): Cambridge University Press.

Cassiman, B., & Veugelers, R. (2002). R&D Cooperation and Spillovers: Some Empirical Evidence from Belgium. *American Economic Review, 92(4),* 1169-1184.

Chaney, T. (2008). Distorted Gravity: the Intensive and Extensive Margins of International Trade. *American Economic Review, 98(4),* 1707-1721.

Coase, R. H. (1937). The Nature of the Firm. *Economica, 4,* 386-405.

Coe, D. T., & Helpman, E. (1995). International R&D Spillovers. *European Economic Review, 39(5),* 859-887.

Coe, D. T., Helpman, E., & Hoffmaister, A. W. (2009). International R&D Spillovers and Institutions. *European Economic Review, 53(7),* 723-741.

Cohen, W. M., & Klepper, S. (1996). Firm Size and the Nature of Innovation Within Industries: The Case of Process and Product R&D. *Review of Economics & Statistics, 78(2),* 232-243.

Colombo, M. G., & Grilli, L. (2005). Founders' Human Capital and the Growth of New Technology-based Firms -A Competence-based View. *Research Policy, 34(6),* 795-816.

Corrado, C., Hulten, C., & Sichel, D. (2009). Intangible Capital and U.S. Economic Growth. *Review of Income and Wealth, 55(3),* 661-685.

Council on Competitiveness. (2004). Innovate America. http://www. compete. org/publications/detail/202/innovate-america/

Dekle, R., Eaton, J., & Kortum., S. (2008). Global Rebalancing with Gravity: Measuring the Burden of Adjustment. IMF Staff Papers, 55 (3), 511-540.

Diewert, W. E., Greenlees, J. S., & Hulten, C. R. (2009). *Price Index Concepts and Measurement*: University of Chicago Press.

Dikaiakos, M. D., Katsaros, D., Mehra, P., Pallis, G., & Vakali, A. (2009). Cloud Computing: Distributed Internet Computing for IT and Scientific Research. *IEEE Internet Computing, 13(5),* 10-13.

Djellal, F., Francoz, D., Gallouj, C., Gallouj, F., & Jacquin, Y. (2003). Revising the Definition of Research and Development in the Light of the Specificities of Services. *Science and Public Policy, 30,* 415-429.

Dosi, G. (1988). Sources, Procedures, and Microeconomic Effects of Innovation. *Journal of Economic Literature, 26(3),* 1120-1171.

Duchêne, V., Lykogianni, E., & Verbeek, A. (2009). EU R&D in Services Industries and the EU-US R&D Investment Gap. http://iri.jrc.ec. europa.eu/papers/04_IPTS_WP_JRC50911.pdf

Dunham, D. (2003). Products, Innovations and Productivity. *Medical Laboratory Observer,* Nov 22-23 issue.

Dunne, T. (1994). Plant Age and Technology Use in U.S. Manufacturing Industries. *RAND Journal of Economics, 25(3),* 488-499.

EU Scientific and Technical Research Committee. (2008). CREST Conclusions on R&D in Services – Review and Case Studies: Promoting the Role of Systematic R&D in Services. http://register.consilium. europa.eu/pdf/en/08/st01/st01205.en08.pdf

Eaton, J., Kortum, S., & Kramarz, F. (2009). *An Anatomy of International Trade -Evidence from French Firms*: Center for Economic Policy Research.

Eaton, J. & Kortum, S. (2002). Technology, Geography, and Trade, *Econometrica, 70(5),* 1741-1779.

Einstein, A. (1949). Why Socialism? *Monthly Review,* May.

Enterprise index. Statistics Denmark. http://www.dst.dk/

Ericson, R., & Pakes, A. (1995). Markov-perfect Industry Dynamics: A Framework for Empirical Work. *Review of Economic Studies, 62(210),* 53-82.

Essama-Nssah, B. (2007). A Poverty-Focused Evaluation of Commodity Tax Options. World Bank Policy Research Working Paper No. 4245: World Bank.

European Commission. The Observatory of European SMEs. http://ec.europa. eu/enterprise/policies/sme/facts-figures-analysis/sme-observatory/index_en.htm

European Commission. (2008). R&D in Services – Review and Case Studies. A paper submitted for the CREST. http://ec.europa.eu/invest-in-research/pdf/download_en/service_rd080129.pdf

European Commission. (2009). Preparing Europe for a New Renaissance -A Strategic View of the European Research Area. http://ec.europa.eu/ research/erab/pdf/erab-first-annual-report-06102009_en.pdf

Eurostat. (1992-2009). Community Innovation Survey (CIS). http://cordis.europa.eu/innovation/en/policy/cis.htm.

Eurostat. (2007). Eurostat Statistics on Human Resources in Science and Technology (HRST). http://epp.eurostat.ec.europa.eu/ portal/page/portal/ science_technology_innovation/data/database

Eurostat. (2008). Employment in knowledge-intensive service sectors: Share of total employment (%). http://epp.eurostat.ec.europa.eu/ tgm/table.do?tab=table&init=1&plugin=1&language=en&pcode=tsc0001 2

Federal Statistics Office of Germany. http://www.destatis.de/ jetspeed/ portal/cms/Sites/destatis/Internet/EN/Navigation/Homepage__NT.psml

Finnish Funding Agency for Technology and Innovation (TeKes). (2006). Serve - Innovative Services Technology Programme 2006-2010. http://akseli.tekes.fi/opencms/opencms/OhjelmaPortaali/ohjelmat/Serve/en /etusivu.html.

Finnish Funding Agency for Technology and Innovation (TeKes). (2007a). Productivity of Business Services – Towards a New Taxonomy. http://akseli.tekes.fi/opencms/opencms/OhjelmaPortaali/ohjelmat/Serve/fi/ Dokumenttiarkisto/Viestinta_ja_aktivointi/Julkaisut/Productivity_of_busi ness_services.pdf

Finnish Funding Agency for Technology and Innovation (TeKes). (2007b). Seizing the White Space: Innovative Service Concepts in the United States. http://akseli.tekes.fi/opencms/opencms/Ohjelma Portaali/ ohjelmat/Serve/fi/Dokumenttiarkisto/Viestinta_ja_aktivointi/Julkaisut/Sei zing_the_White_Space_Innovative_service.pdf

Finnish Funding Agency for Technology and Innovation (TeKes). (2007c). Serve -Innovative Internationally competitive business from service innovations. http://www.tekes.fi/serve.

Fishman, A., & Rob, R. (1999). The Size of Firms and R&D Investment. *International Economic Review, 40(4)*, 915-931.

Fontana, R., Geuna, A., & Matt, M. (2006). Factors Affecting University-Industry R&D Projects -The Importance of Searching, Screening and Signaling. *Research Policy, 35(2)*, 309-323.

Forge, S., Blackman, C., Bohlin, E., & Cave, M. (2009). A Green Knowledge Society -An ICT Policy Agenda to 2015 for Europe's Future Knowledge Society. http://ec.europa.eu/information_society/eeurope/ i2010/greenknowledgesociety.pdf.

Freeman, C., & Louca, F. (2001). *As Times Goes By: From the Industrial Revolutions to the Information Revolution*: Oxford University Press.

Freeman, C., & Soete, L. (1997). *The Economics of Industrial Innovation*: Pinter.

Freeman, C., & Soete, L. (2007). Developing Science, Technology and Innovation Indicators: What We Can Learn From the Past. United Nations University-Merit Working Paper Series No. 2007-001.

Fritsch, M., & Lukas, R. (2001). Who Cooperates on R&D? *Research Policy*, *30(2)*, 297-312.

Fuchs, V. R. (1965). The Growing Importance of the Service Industries. *The Journal of Business*, *38(4)*, 344-373.

Fujita, M., Krugman, P., & Venables, A. J. (2001). *The Spatial Economy: Cities, Regions, and International Trade*: The MIT Press.

Fukao, K. (2007). Productivity in Japan, the US, and the EU Core Countries - Is Japan Falling Behind. RIETI Discussion Paper Series No. 07-E-046, The Research Institute of Economy, Trade and Industry (RIETI).

Georghiou, L. (2003). Foresight - Providing the Strategic Knowledge for Technology Management. Paper presented at Portland International Conference on Management of Engineering and Technology, July 20-24.

Ghironi, F., & Melitz, M. J. (2005). International Trade and Macroeconomic Dynamics with Heterogeneous Firms. *Quarterly Journal of Economics*, *120(3)*, 865-915.

Gibrat, R. (1931). *Les inegalites e'conomiques; applications: aux inegalites des richesses, a la concentration des entreprises, aux populations des villes, aux statistiques des families, etc.,d'une loi nouvelle, la loi de l'effet proportionnel.* Paris: Librairie du Recueil Sirey.

Goldsmith, S., & Eggers, W. D. (2004). *Governing by network -The New Shape of the Public Sector*: Brookings Institution Press and John F Kennedy School of Government at Harvard University.

Griffith, R., Harrison, R., & Van Reenen, J. (2006). How Special Is the Special Relationship? Using the Impact of U.S. R&D Spillovers on U.K. Firms as a Test of Technology Sourcing. *American Economic Review*, *96(5)*, 1859-1875.

Griffith, R., Redding, ‘S., & Van Reenen, J. (2003). R&D and Absorptive Capacity -Theory and Empirical Evidence. *Scandinavian Journal of Economics*, *105(1)*, 99-118.

Griliches, Z. (1994). Productivity, R&D, and the Data Constraint. *American Economic Review*, *84(1)*, 1-23.

Grönroos, C. (1990). Relationship Approach to Marketing in Service Contexts: The Marketing and Organizational Behavior Interface. *Journal of Business Research*, *20(1)*, 3-11.

Grönroos, C. (1999). Relationship Marketing: Challenges for the Organization. *Journal of Business Research*, *46(3)*, 327-335.

Grönroos, C., & Ojasalo, K. (2004). Service Productivity: Towards a Conceptualization of the Transformation of Inputs into Economic Results in Services. *Journal of Business Research*, *57(4)*, 414-423.

Hahn, J., Hausman, J., & Kuersteinerm, G. (2002). Bias Corrected Instrumental Variables Estimation for Dynamic Panel Models with Fixed Effects. Mimeo, MIT.

Hall, B. H. (2007). Measuring the Returns to R&D -The Depreciation Problem. NBER Working Paper Series No. 13473, National Bureau of Economic Research (NBER).

Hall, B. H., Jaffe, A., & Trajtenberg, M. (2001). Market Value and Patent Citations. *RAND Journal of Economics, 36,* 16-38.

Hall, B. H., Thoma, G., & Torrisi, S. (2007). The Market Value of Patents and R&D -Evidence From European Firms. NBER Working Paper No. 13426, National Bureau of Economic Research (NBER).

Hartwig, J. (2008). Productivity Growth in Service Industries -Are the Transatlantic Differences Measurement-Driven? *Review of Income and Wealth, 54(3),* 494-505.

Helpman, E. (2006). Trade, FDI, and the Organization of Firms. *Journal of Economic Literature, 44(3),* 589-630.

Hidaka, K. (2006). Trends in Services Science in Japan and Abroad. *NISTEP Science and Technology Trend Quarterly Review, 19,* 35-47: National Institute of Science and Technology Policy (NISTEP).

Hill, T. P. (1977). On Goods and Services. *Review of Income and Wealth, 23(4),* 315-338.

Hipp, C., & Grupp, H. (2005). Innovation in the Service Sector: The Demand for Service-specific Innovation Measurement Concepts and Typologies. *Research Policy, 34(4),* 517-535.

IBM. Service Science, Management and Engineering. http://www.ibm. com/developerworks/spaces/ssme

Industry Canada. (2005). Key Small Business Statistics. http://www.ic.gc.ca/ eic/site/sbrp-rppe.nsf/eng/h_rd01252.html

International Monetary Fund. (2009a). World Economic Outlook - Crisis and Recovery.

International Monetary Fund. (2009b). World Economy Outlook - Sustaining the Recovery.

Ishaq, N. M., & Prucha, I. R. (1996). Estimation of the Depreciation Rate of Physical and R&D Capital in the U.S. Total Manufacturing Sector. *Economic Inquiry, 34(1),* 43-56.

Jaffe, A. B., Trajtenberg, M., & Fogarty, M. S. (2000). Knowledge Spillovers and Patent Citations: Evidence from a Survey of Inventors. *American Economic Review, 90(2),* 215-218.

Jankowski, J. E. (2001). Measurement and Growth of R&D Within the Service Economy. *The Journal of Technology Transfer, 26(4)*, 323-336.

Japan Statistics Bureau. Economic Census. http://www.stat. go.jp/english/data/ index.htm

Jensen, J. B., Kletzer, L. G., Bernstein, J., & Feenstra, R. C. (2005). Tradable Services -Understanding the Scope and Impact of Services Offshoring. Brookings Trade Forum, Offshoring White-Collar Work, 75-133. The Brookings Institution.

Jonathan, E., & Samuel, K. (2002). Technology, Geography, and Trade. *Econometrica, 70(5)*, 1741-1779.

Jorgenson, D. W., Ho, M. S., & Stiroh, K. J. (2003). Lessons from the US Growth Resurgence. *Journal of Policy Modeling, 25*, 453–470.

Kasahara, H., & Lapham, B. J. (2008). Productivity and the Decision to Import and Export: Theory and Evidence. CESifo Working Paper No. 2240, CESifo Group Munich.

Kasahara, H., & Rodrigue, J. (2008). Does the Use of Imported Intermediates Increase Productivity? Plant-level evidence. *Journal of Development Economics, 87(1)*, 106-118.

Kinoshita, Y. (2009a). Analysis of Macro-micro Simulation Models for Service-oriented Public Platform. In C. Godart, N. Gronau, S. Sharma, & G. Canals (Eds.), *Software Services for e-Business and e-Society* (pp. 328–340): Springer.

Kinoshita, Y. (2009b). Review on the Qualitative Measurement Methodology of Innovation in Service Using Panel Data. Paper presented at JASI/JSIS Joint Annual Conference, 220-225. The Japan Association for Social Informatics (JASI) and the Japan Society for Socio-information Studies (JSIS).

Kinoshita, Y., & Sudoh, O. (2008). Network-driven Context in User-driven Innovation. In M. Oya, R. Uda, & C. Yasunobu (Eds.), *Towards Sustainable Society on Ubiquitous Networks* (pp. 245-252): Springer.

Klette, T. J., & Griliches, Z. (2000). Empirical Patterns of Firm Growth and R&D Investment -A Quality Ladder Model Interpretation. *The Economic Journal, 110(463)*, 363-387.

Klette, T. J., & Kortum, S. (2004). Innovating Firms and Aggregate Innovation. *Journal of Political Economy, 112(5)*, 986-1018.

Koeller, C. T. (1995). Innovation, Market Structure and Firm Size -A Simultaneous Equations Model. *Journal of Managerial and Decision Economics, 16(3)*, 259-269.

Koeller, C. T. (2005). Technological Opportunity and the Relationship Between Innovation Output and Market Structure. *Journal of Managerial and Decision Economics, 26(3)*, 209-222.

Koellinger, P. (2008). The Relationship Between Technology, Innovation, and Firm Performance -Empirical Evidence From e-Business In Europe. *Research Policy, 37(8)*, 1317-1328.

Kozak, M. (2007). Micro, Small, and Medium Enterprises -A Collection of Published Data. International Finance Corporation. http://rru.worldbank.org/Documents/other/MSMEdatabase/msme_database.htm

Kranich, J. (2009). Agglomeration, Innovation and International Research Mobility. *Economic Modeling, 26(5)*, 817-830.

Krugman, P. (1989). Industrial organization and international trade. In R. Schmalensee & R. Willig (Eds.), *Handbook of Industrial Organization* (Vol 2, pp. 1179-1223): Elsevier.

Krugman, P. (1997). *Development, Geography, and Economic Theory*: MIT Press.

Kuusisto, J. (2008a). R&D in Services - Review and Case Studies. DG Research, European Commission.

Kuusisto, J. (2008b). Towards High Performance Services - Implications for Innovation Policy, a Review of Research Literature. Presented at High-Level Roundtable on Innovation in Services, Brussels, Nov 27.

Kuusisto, J., & Viljamaa, A. (2006). System Competence as Prerequisite of SME's Ability to Benefit from Policy Instruments. SC-Research. http://www.sc-research.fi/downloads/301_Ref_B139.pdf

Lages, L. F., & Fernandes, J. C. (2005). The SERPVAL scale -A multi-item instrument for measuring service personal values. *Journal of Business Research, 58(11)*, 1562-1572.

Lelarge, C. (2009). The Innovative Activity of Firms Over Their Life Cycle Evidence from French Micro-Data: OECD DSTI/ES and CREST-INSEE.

Levinsohn, J., & Petrin, A. (2003). Estimating Production Functions Using Inputs to Control for Unobservables. *Review of Economic Studies, 70(243)*, 317-341.

Lotti, F., Santarelli, E., & Vivarelli, M. (2009). Defending Gibrat's Law as a Long-run Regularity. *Small Business Economics, 32(1)*, 31-44.

López, A. (2008). Determinants of R&D Cooperation: Evidence from Spanish Manufacturing Firms. *International Journal of Industrial Organization, 26(1)*, 113-136.

Lööf, H., & Heshmati, A. (2002). Knowledge Capital and Performance Heterogeneity: An Innovation Study at Firm Level. *International Journal of Production Economics, 76(1)*, 61-85.

Mansfield, E. (1968). *Industrial Research and Technological Change*: W.W. Norton & Company.

Melitz, M. J. (2003). The Impact of Trade on Intra-Industry Reallocations and Aggregate Industry Productivity. *Econometrica, 71(6)*, 1695-1725.

Miles, I. (2005). Knowledge Intensive Business Services: *Prospects and Policies. Foresight, 7(6)*, 39-63.

Miles, I. (2006). Innovation in Services. In J. Fagerberg, D. C. Mowery & R. R. Nelson (Eds.), *The Oxford Handbook of Innovation* (pp. 433-458): Oxford University Press.

Miles, I. (2007). Research and Development (R&D) Beyond Manufacturing - The Strange Case of Services R&D. *R&D Management, 37(3)*, 249-268.

Miles, I. (2008). Patterns of Innovation in Service Industries. *IBM Systems Journal, 47(1)*, 115-128.

Miotti, L., & Sachwald, F. (2003). Co-operative R&D: Why and With Whom? -An Integrated Framework of Analysis. *Research Policy, 32(8)*, 1481-1499.

Miozzo, M., & Soete, L. (2001). Internationalization of Services -A Technological Perspective. *Technological Forecasting and Social Change, 67*, 159-185.

Mohnen, P., & Hoareau, C. (2003). What Type of Enterprise Forges Close Links With Universities and Government Labs? Evidence from CIS 2. *Managerial and Decision Economics, 24(2-3)*, 133-145.

Morikawa, M. (2010). Instability of Business Performance and Part-time Workers (Original title in Japanese: *Kigyo gyoseki no fuantei sei to hiseiki roudou*). RIETI Discussion Paper Series No. 10-J-023, The Research Institute of Economy, Trade and Industry (RIETI).

Motohashi, K. (2005). University-Industry Collaborations in Japan: The Role of New Technology-Based Firms in Transforming the National Innovation System. *Research Policy, 34(5)*, 583-594.

Mueller, D. C. (1967). The Firm Decision Process: An Econometric Investigation. *Journal of Political Economy, 81*, 58–87.

Mulkay, B., Hall, B. H., & Mairesse, J. (2001). Firm Level Investment and R&D in France and the United States -A Comparison. Economic Papers No. 2001-W2, Economics Group, Nuffield College, University of Oxford.

NESTA Policy and Research Unit. (2008). Innovation in Services. Policy Briefing. The National Endowment for Science, Technology and the Arts

(NESTA). http://www.nesta.org.uk/assets/Uploads/pdf/Policy-Briefing/ innovation_in_services_policy_briefing_NESTA.pdf

NISTEP. (2008). Study for the Development of Innovation Measurement Methodology: National Institute of Science and Technology Policy (NISTEP).

NISTEP. (2009). Economic Analysis of Innovation: National Institute of Science and Technology Policy (NISTEP).

National Institute for Economic and Social Research, & Groningen Growth and Development Centre. (1970-2008). KLEMS Growth and Productivity Accounts. European Union. http://www.euklems.net

National Institute of Statistics and Economic Studies of France. http://www.insee.fr/en/

National Science Foundation and National Institute of Standards and Technology. (2005). Measuring Service-Sector Research and Development -Final Report. Planning report No. 05-1, U.S. Department of Commerce.

Nevo, A., & Rosen, A. M. (2008). Identification with Imperfect Instruments. NBER Working Paper No. 14434, The National Bureau of Economic Research (NBER).

Nomura, K. (2004). *Measurement of Capital and Productivity in Japan*: Keio University Press.

OECD. (1980). Frascati Manual -The Measurement of Scientific and Technical Activities.

OECD. (1990-2007). Research and Development Expenditure in Industry (ANBERD).

OECD. (1992). Oslo manual -The measurement of scientific and technological activities, Proposed guidelines for collecting and interpreting technological innovation data.

OECD. (1996). Services -Measuring Real Annual Value Added.

OECD. (2002). SME and Entrepreneurship Outlook.

OECD. (2005a). Enhancing the Performance of Service Activities.

OECD. (2005b). Oslo Manual -Guidelines for Collecting and Interpreting Innovation Data (3rd ed.): OECD and Eurostat.

OECD. (2005c). SME and Entrepreneurship Outlook.

OECD. (2006). Innovation and Knowledge-Intensive Service Activities.

OECD. (2008a). Enhancing the Role of SMEs in Global Value Chains.

OECD. (2008b). Glossary of Statistical Terms.

OECD. (2008c). Information and Technology Outlook.

OECD. (2008d). Removing Barriers to SME Access to International Markets.

OECD. (2008e). STAN Database for Structural Analysis.

OECD. (2009a). Main Science and Technology Indicators.

OECD (2009b). Factbook –Economic, Environmental and Social Statistics.

OECD. (2009c). OECD Factbook eXplorer.

OECD. Business Statistics by Size Class (BSC).

OECD. Statistics on Business Demography (BD).

OECD. Statistics on Enterprises by Size Class (SEC).

OECD. Structural Statistics for Industry and Services (SSIS).

OECD. Structural and Demographics Business Statistics (SDBS).

Ohashi, H. (2007). How to Measure the Outcome of Innovations: Application to Product Innovations. Paper prepared for Toward Global Innovation Ecosystem.

Okamuro, H., Honjo, Y., & Kato, M. (2009). Determinants of Research Partnership Formation by Japanese High-tech Start-ups. Paper presented at Comparative Analysis of Enterprise (Micro) Data Conference. http://gcoe.ier.hit-u.ac.jp/CAED/papers/id207_Okamuro_Honjo_ Kato. pdf

Olley, G. S., & Pakes, A. (1996). The Dynamics of Productivity in the Telecommunications Equipment Industry. *Econometrica, 64(6),* 1263-1297.

Ottaviano, G. I. P., & Melitz, M. J. (2008). Market Size, Trade, and Productivity. *Review of Economic Studies, 75(1),* 295-316.

PREST, TNO, ARCS, & SERVILAB. (2006). The Future Of R&D in Services -Implications for EU Research and Innovation Policy. A report commissioned by the Science and Technology Foresight Unit of DG. ftp://ftp.cordis.europa.eu/pub/foresight/docs/ntw_conf_services_report-en.pdf

Pagano, P., & Schivardi, F. (2003). Firm Size Distribution and Growth. Scandinavian *Journal of Economics, 105(2),* 255-274.

Pakes, A. (2003). Common Sense and Simplicity in Empirical Industrial Organization. *Review of Industrial Organization, 23(3),* 193-215.

Pakes, A., & Ericson, R. (1998). Empirical Implications of Alternative Models of Firm Dynamics. *Journal of Economic Theory, 79(1),* 1-45.

Pakes, A., & Griliches, Z. (1980). Patents and R&D at the Firm Level -A First Report. *Economics Letters, 5(4),* 377-381.

Pakes, A., & Schankerman, M. (1979). The Rate of Obsolescence of Knowledge, Research Gestation Lags, and the Private Rate of Return to Research Resources, NBER Working Paper Series No. 0346, National Bureau of Economic Research (NBER).

Patrizio, P., & Fabiano, S. (2003). Firm Size Distribution and Growth. Scandinavian *Journal of Economics, 105(2)*, 255-274.

Rimal, B. P., Eunmi, C., & Lumb, I. (2009). A Taxonomy and Survey of Cloud Computing Systems. Paper presented at International Conference on Networked Computing and Advanced Information Management, 44-51.

SMEs in New Zealand (SME statistics), New Zealand Ministry of Economic Development. http://www.med.govt.nz/templates/Content TopicSummary____39289.aspx

Sargent, T. J., & Williams, N. (2005). Impacts of Priors on Convergence and Escapes from Nash Inflation. *Review of Economic Dynamics, 8(2)*, 360-391.

Sasser, W. E., Olsen, R. P., & Wyckoff, D. D. (1978). *Management of Service Operations*: Allyn & Bacon.

Schankerman, M., & Pakes, A. (1986). Estimates of the Value of Patent Rights in European Countries During the Post-1950 Period. *Economic Journal, 96(384)*, 1052-1076.

Scherer, F. M. (1983). The Propensity to Patent. *International Journal of Industrial Organization, 1(1)*, 107-128.

Schwalbach, J., & Zimmermann, K. F. (1991). A Poisson Model of Patenting and Firm Structure in Germany. In Z. Acs & D. B. Audretsch (Eds.), *Innovation and Technological Change -An International Comparison*: University of Michigan Press.

Scott, D. (2010). The Adverse Feedback Loop and the Real Effects of Financial Sector Uncertainty. Paper presented at the Sixth Dynare Conference. Bank of Finland, DSGE-net and Dynare Project at CEPREMAP.

Scott, J. T. (1999). The Service Sector's Acquisition and Development of Information Technology: Infrastructure and Productivity. *The Journal of Technology Transfer, 24(1)*, 37-54.

Second OECD Ad Hoc Meeting on Biotechnology Statistics. (2001). Biotechnology -List-based Definition: OECD. http://stats.oecd.org/ glossary/detail.asp?ID=218

Service Innovation Research Initiative. (2009). Proposal Towards the Establishment of an Informatical Foundation of Services to Realize Innovation: Division of University Corporate Relations, the University of Tokyo.http://www.ducr.u-tokyo.ac.jp/service-innovation/pdf/ 090331teigen-en.pdf

Shapiro, C., Varian, H. R., & Farrel, J. (2004). *The Economics of Information Technology -An Introduction*: Cambridge University Press.

Shefer, D., & Frenkel, A. (2005). R&D, Firm Size and Innovation: An Empirical Analysis. *Technovation, 25(1)*, 25-32.

Small Business Forum of Ireland. (2005). Report of the Small Business Forum. http://www.smallbusinessforum.ie/

Small and Medium Enterprise Agency. (2004-2008). Survey of SMEs Business Activity. http://www.chusho.meti.go.jp/sme_english/index. html

Small and Medium Enterprise Statistics for the UK and Regions (1994-2008). Department for Business, Innovation and Skills, UK National Statistics. http://stats.bis.gov.uk/ed/sme/

State Secretariat for Economic Affairs of Switzerland. http://www. seco.admin.ch/index.html?lang=en

Stauning, S. (2007). Establishing a National Service Oriented eBusiness and eGovernment Infrastructure. OASIS Symposium, April 15-20, San Diego, California.

Stiroh, K. J. (2002). Information Technology and the U.S. Productivity Revival: What Do the Industry Data Say? *American Economic Review, 92(5),* 1559-1576.

Sudoh, O. (2005). The Knowledge Network in the Digital Economy and Sustainable Development. In O. Sudoh (Ed.), *Digital Economy and Social Design* (pp. 3-38): Springer.

Sudoh, O. (2006). *Coping with Information Explosion: Need to Build a New Social Infrastructure.* Glocom Platform. http://www.glocom.org/ opinions/essays/20060814_sudoh_coping

Sudoh, O. (2008). Administrative Evolution and Open Innovation. *Journal of Social Informatics Research, 1(1)*, 147-160.

Tether, B. S. (2002). Who Co-operates for Innovation, and Why: An Empirical Analysis. *Research Policy, 31(6)*, 947-967.

Timmer, M. P., O'Mahony, M., & Ark, B. V. (2007). *EU KLEMS Growth and Productivity Accounts: Overview* (Nov 2007 Release). EU KLEMS Project.

Triplett, J. E., & Bosworth, B. P. (2004). *Services Productivity in the United States -New Sources of Economic Growth*: Brookings Institution Press.

Tsai, K.H., & Wang, J.C. (2005). Does R&D Performance Decline with Firm Size? -A Re-examination in Terms of Elasticity. *Research Policy, 34,* 966-976.

U.S. Census Bureau. Economic Census of Island Areas. http://www.census. gov/econ/islandareas/

U.S. Census Bureau. Statistics of U.S. Businesses. http://www.census.gov/econ/susb/

U.S. Economic Classification Policy Committee (ECPC), Statistics Canada, and Mexico's Instituto Nacional de Estadistica, Geografia e Informatica (1997). North American Industry Classification System (NAICS). http://www.census.gov/eos/www/naics/

UK Office for National Statistics. SME Statistics for the UK. http://stats.berr.gov.uk/ed/sme

United Nations Economic Commission for Europe. (2003). Small and Medium-Sized Enterprises in Countries in Transition. http://www.insme.org/documents/Small%20and%20MediumSized%20Enterprises%20in%20Countries%20in%20Transition.pdf

United Nations Statistics Division. International Standard Industrial Classification (ISIC): United Nations. http://unstats.un.org/unsd/cr/registry/regct.asp

Veugelers, R., & Cassiman, B. (2005). R&D Cooperation Between Firms and Universities. Some Empirical Evidence from Belgian Manufacturing. International *Journal of Industrial Organization, 23(5-6),* 355-379.

Wolfl, A. (2005). The Service Economy in OECD Countries. OECD Science, Technology and Industry Working Papers No. 2005/3: OECD Publishing.

World Bank. (2008). Global Development Finance -The Role of International Banking.

World Bank. (2009). Global Economic Prospects -Commodities at the Crossroads: The International Bank for Reconstruction and Development.

World Trade Organization. (2009). Statistics Database -Time Series on International Trade.

Yasar, M. (2008). Production function estimation in Stata using the Olley and Pakes method. *Stata Journal, 8(2),* 221-231.

Yoshikawa, H. & Miyakawa, N. (2009). Industrial Structural Change and the Growth of the Japanese Economy in the Post-war Period (Original title in Japanese: *Sangyo-kouzou no henka to sengo nihon no keizai seicho*). RIETI Discussion Paper Series No. 09-J-024, The Research Institute of Economy, Trade and Industry (RIETI).

Young, A. (1996). *Measuring R&D in the Services*: OECD Publishing.

Yu, J., Li, M., Li, Y., & Hong, F. (2004). An Economy-Based Accounting System for Grid Computing Environments. Paper presented at International Workshop on Web Information Systems, 233-238: Springer.

Zeithaml, V. A., Parasuraman, A., & Berry, L. L. (1990). *Delivering Quality Service -Balancing Customer Perceptions and Expectations*: Free Press.

Zellner, A. (2008). Bayesian econometrics: Past, Present, and Future. In S. Chib, W. Griffiths, G. Koop, and D. Terrell (Eds.), *Bayesian Econometrics*: Emerald Group Publishing.

INDEX